MW01195086

"I loved *The Frog Whispe*
easy-to-follow process fr
prince. Filled with humor, ... exercises,
this book is bound to help you leap into the arms of your true love."

Debi Berndt, Author of *Let Love In: Open Your Heart
& Mind to Attract Your Ideal Partner* (Wiley)

"Jane provides singles with a road map for getting to what they ultimately want, LOVE! Moving past our barriers is absolutely essential.
This book offers a step-by-step for doing just that!"

Colin Tipping, Author of *Radical Forgivness*

"*The Frog Whisperer* is a fun and thoughtful read!"

Mary LoVerde, Author of *The Invitation*

"When Jane Atkinson speaks or writes, I listen, read and learn. Her
wisdom and understanding is beyond her years. She is a success on
many fronts and that's how we grow, learning from successful people.
I have and so will you."

Peter Legge, Author of *The Power of a Dream*

"I loved it, couldn't put it down."

Nancy Michienzi, London, Ontario

The Frog
Whisperer

The Frog Whisperer

A 3-Step
Approach
to Finding
Lasting Love

JANE ATKINSON

LIVE OAK
BOOK COMPANY

www.liveoakbookcompany.com

Published by Live Oak Book Company
Austin, TX
www.liveoakbookcompany.com

Copyright ©2011 Jane Atkinson

All rights reserved.

No part of this book may be reproduced, stored in a retrieval system, or transmitted by any means, electronic, mechanical, photocopying, recording, or otherwise, without written permission from the copyright holder.

Distributed by Live Oak Book Company

For ordering information or special discounts for bulk purchases, please contact Live Oak Book Company at PO Box 91869, Austin, TX 78709, 512.891.6100.

Design and composition by Kim Monteforte, WeMakeBooks.ca
Cover design by Dana Koch, Koch Ink and Kim Monteforte,
     WeMakeBooks.ca
Interior graphics © Julien Tromeur, Dreamstime.com

Cataloging-in-Publication data
(Prepared by The Donohue Group, Inc.)

Atkinson, Jane (Jane Elizabeth), 1964–
     The frog whisperer : a 3-step approach to finding lasting love /
     Jane Atkinson. — 1st ed.

p. ; cm.

Issued also as an ebook.

ISBN: 978-1-936909-30-8

1. Dating (social customs) 2. Man-woman relationships. 3. Love.
I. Title.

HQ801 .A85 2012

306.73   2011939895

First Edition

First, thank you to John for coming into my life and being an incredible man and husband. Thank you to my parents, married 62 years, always a source of inspiration and encouragement. And thanks to my amazing book team who made this project feel less like work and more like fun!

CONTENTS

HOME Jane and John Today 135

Hawaii: Party of Two

My new husband and I boarded the flight to Maui with anticipation. On some level, we both knew this trip was going to be one of the most memorable in our lives. Using the "It's our honeymoon" line, we scored excellent seats right up front. Although not technically in first class, the flight attendants chatted with us and gave us VIP treatment the entire flight. We had a blast. At times we were cozy and romantic; closer to arrival, we were drinking champagne and laughing with everyone. It was the perfect beginning.

We landed on time, picked up our convertible rental car and set out for Napili on the northwest side of the island where our ocean-side condo awaited. My maid of honor's husband was from Hawaii and his mom was sweet enough to offer her luxury suite to us for 10 days! As we drove down the winding highway, thick with tropical vegetation, we were impressed, but when we saw the blue sparkling water of the bay, we were blown away. Within minutes we saw whales. Their shimmering black and white bodies, most weighing more than a ton, were the most extraordinary vision as they rose from the water. It was as if they were all out in the bay just to greet us, breaching and splashing around only for our amusement.

This was my second trip to Hawaii. The first time was 18 years ago. I was 25 and solo, stopping over on my way to Australia. I stayed in hostels and met a few people, but that trip seemed hollow and colorless in comparison to this one.

Now I was in Hawaii with the love of my life. My husband!

At the age of 43, I could honestly say I really wasn't sure Mr. Right would ever come along. I had always told myself that when I was ready, truly ready, it would happen. But as the years had ticked by, I started to wonder, "Would I ever meet The One?"

Thankfully, I did.

When we arrived at our condo and settled into our room, I sat on the bed and looked out at the ocean to absorb the beautiful scene. I shouted almost immediately, "Honey, come quick! There are whales right here! Hurry!!"

I had seen a mother and a baby whale playing together right offshore. He rushed in, wrapped his arms around me and we watched those magnificent whales for an hour in complete awe.

For the first time in my life I had someone else to share an extraordinary moment with and it was pure heaven. I had traveled the world and seen many unbelievable sights, but I will never forget those amazing moments.

Finding my perfect mate has been a huge turning point in my life. Allowing love in took some time (and a whole bunch of frogs) but it was 100% worth it!

Perhaps reading this book will be the beginning of a new chapter in your life. Do you think?

Frog Whispering

If you've ever seen *The Dog Whisperer* on TV, you'll know that canine expert Cesar Millan has a really interesting approach to human-dog relationships. His theory: it's often the human who is creating the problem, not the dog. The human's energy toward the dog or a situation can result in bad behavior. The human is putting out a negative, frightened, or frustrated vibe and the dog is simply responding to that vibe.

I believe relationships among humans are similar: it's the energy that we put out to the world that creates both bad and good results. If your mantra is "There are no good men left out there," that may just become your reality. However, if you feel great about yourself and move into the world with an "I'm fabulous! Men, come on down and meet me!" attitude, you may find your results more positive.

"Every thought is a seed. If you plant crab apples, don't count on harvesting Golden Delicious."
– Bill Meyer

A man named Bill Meyer once said, "Every thought is a seed. If you plant crab apples, don't count on harvesting Golden Delicious."

When we attain a state of happiness within ourselves (loving ourselves) prior to finding love with another, we'll be putting out the best vibe possible. In turn, that will bring more suitable prospects to our door.

The Frog Whisperer is not about controlling the "Frogs," the people you date; it's about aligning with your best self and being as happy as possible so that you don't have to kiss frogs anymore!

Is there a Prince or Princess out there for you? I don't buy into most fairy tale concepts but I do believe in "happily ever after." And yes, I believe your perfect mate – someone who is right for you – is out there. John is my proof. He has been my knight in shining armor on many occasions. But hey, he didn't save me; I saved myself first, and then he came along.

> *He didn't save me; I saved myself first, and then he came along.*

Your Blueprint for Love

In today's high tech world, if someone has decided they want to find love, the first step they take is to post a profile on a dating site. (I realize some are too skeptical or shy for this, but it's becoming the "norm.") Sometimes they get lucky, but many spend years trying different sites, dating different people and never having success.

If you're building a house, you don't just start randomly digging up the ground. You have specs, drawings and a time line in place. So why, when we decide we want love in our life, do we just dive right in?

My own painful experience of kissing frog after frog, year after year, is the reason this book came to life. I made the decision that I needed to stop and create a plan before posting a profile if anything were ever going to change for me. Guess what? It worked! And *The Frog Whisperer* concept was born.

The Results Approach

The Frog Whisperer approach involves three steps: READY, SET, LEAP.

> Ready spells out what your perfect life (including the partner you desire) looks like. It allows you to create the ideal vision. It takes a little self-examination.
>
> Set is what you need to do to become the best version of your-self. Most of us have some issues that are holding us back and resolving them will help. This will be the big work phase.
>
> Leap takes you out into the dating world with some tools to use. Knowing what you are looking for, from a values perspective, will come into play here.

This approach will help you avoid my pain of kissing frog after frog with the same results, and will allow you to move past your barriers toward lasting love.

No book can promise that you are going to live happily ever after, but I do strongly believe that if you are willing to do the work, you can set yourself up for success.

Getting Ready

I had a very good life before I met John. I had good friends and a strong family, my business was successful and profitable, and I could travel all over the world. I owned a condo that I adored, and I enjoyed the luxury of working from home. To be closer to my parents, who were getting older and needed me more, I moved back to my hometown after years of travel and work.

But, there was still a gaping hole.

When I traveled, I missed having someone to share the wonder of new places with. When I returned home, no one met me at the terminal. When I went to bed every night, there was no one to say, "I love you, babe."

All the money, friends and fun in the world wouldn't, and couldn't, fill that hole.

I was determined to make an important change. In this book I'll outline some of the steps I took to create the life I wanted, and I'll share some of the mistakes I made in getting there. I'll reveal some of my finer Frog moments (see Frog Stories), and the lessons I learned from each of those *mostly* wonderful men.

But my stories come from my perspective only. So I've gathered together some stories of friends and colleagues to demonstrate the variety of experiences. These Success Stories come from all of life's situations and circumstances.

Also sprinkled throughout *The Frog Whisperer* you'll find exercises to help you work through issues and develop a plan. At the end of each step there are a few Ideas to Ponder. You may also find *The Frog Whisperer Journal* helpful. It holds Exercises, Tips and Ideas to Ponder in addition to the ones you'll find in these pages, and provides you room to jot down some of your own ideas and thoughts on your journey. We've also created a relaxation CD, *The Frog Whisperer Positive Practice*, designed to help you get into a positive mental space. You can use it over and over again to help move you into a place of true happiness.

I am writing this book as a reporter, not just of my own life experiences, but of others as well, and I hope their stories, and mine, will inspire you to READY yourself, get SET, and then LEAP.

Near the end, I'll share with you what my life is like today – after the journey. If I have done my job correctly, you will be well on your way to designing the life that is perfect for you.

Author's Note: All stories are based on actual people and facts, but some names and details may have been changed for privacy reasons. My story is based on the "Female Seeks Male" experience, and that's the perspective that this comes from, but that's not to say you couldn't benefit from *The Frog Whisperer* approach if you are a male seeking a female or are someone seeking a same-sex relationship. Love comes in all shapes, sizes, colors and situations; please adjust the ideas to suit yours!

PS: Rinse and Repeat

There's a saying that goes something like, "When the student is ready, the teacher appears." And you might read this book the first time and not embrace it. That's okay. I hope you'll keep it around in case a need arises some time in the future. In fact, my deepest desire would be to see your copy of *The Frog Whisperer* with dog-ears, post-its and highlighter throughout. I hope you'll keep it nearby as a companion whenever you are getting ready to LEAP onto the dating scene.

STEP 1 – READY

Life By Design, Not Accident

"You know you're in love when you can't fall asleep
because reality is finally better than your dreams."
Dr. Seuss

Imagine you are having a perfect day. Not a major milestone day, like a wedding day, just a regular day.

You wake up feeling peaceful and content, look out the window and feel in awe of the scene and your surroundings. You are happy to live here and, for the first time in your life, there is no place else you would rather be.

Your spouse has greeted you with love and asked what you're planning for the day. When you tell him, it excites you because you are spending your time doing exactly what you want to be doing. You are not a slave to others' wants and needs.

Later in the day, you have special plans with your partner and they make you feel a bit giddy. It's something you've been wanting to do for a long time.

Your relationship is solid and has been for many years. Your partner makes you feel special and loved. You have a level of commitment and comfort you never thought possible. You truly feel accepted – flaws and all.

You and your partner flow through life as a team, moving through family drama, work issues and money matters with relative ease. Your yin and yang are in balance and most of the time your strengths work well with his weaknesses.

The two of you travel together, but love coming home just as much. Your hobbies and interests blend together well and your ideas on how to spend your free time are truly compatible.

Does that kind of day sound wonderful to you?

Why wait for life to happen to you by accident? Why not design it?

Many people, both single and married, can only dream about having the perfect day. I believe it's up to you to design your perfect day, and heck, your perfect life. But how can you create it, unless you know precisely what you want?

Exercise 1*

Your Perfect Day and Life with Your Partner

Imagine what a day would be. What would it look like? What are you doing? Who are you seeing? What's around you? Take out your *Frog Whisperer Journal* or use the space below and write it all down. And really get clear on how you want to spend your time – daily and every day.

For example, if you're retired, do you really want a partner who still works? Or, let's say you're in your 40s and you no longer want to go out to the bars drinking all the time, do you really want a partner who loves that scene? Another example is my friend Kara, who is a total outdoors buff. She really doesn't want to attract a couch potato.

* Find this exercise on pages 19 to 21 of *The Frog Whisperer Journal*.

Before beginning a life with someone else, contemplate what you would love your perfect days to look like. For example, for some (like me) hanging out at the beach all day might be ideal, while for others, hitting galleries in the city followed by dinner at a 5-star restaurant might be the perfect day. You might list it all in a long dialogue or document it hour by hour. Describe a perfect day as if it's already true (your brain doesn't know any different). For example, you might write, "We walk hand in hand down the beach each night before sunset and then sit with a glass of wine as the sun sinks into the water." Sometimes you need to get specific on the small things before you can think of the bigger picture. Consider your life a blank canvas, and you are the artist with paintbrush in hand.

The more you write about how your perfect days will look – the clearer you are – the more readily you'll recognize an imperfect match.

Knowing You're Ready

Assessing where you are emotionally at any point in *The Frog Whisperer* process will be the key to moving from step to step. So what are some situations/signs that will indicate you are ready? They'll be different for everyone, but we'll explore the basics to get ready.

You need to know what characteristics you are looking for and what values are important to you so that you can recognize "Mr/Ms Right." If you have any lingering wounds – who doesn't – you need to acknowledge these so that you can work on them in Step 2. It's also important that you learn to recognize the "dating wounded" so you can become a partner and not a savior.

The signs of readiness will be different for everyone. I'll provide some examples from my friends and myself, but it really boils down to an awareness of yourself, often in the form of patterns.

"Definition of Insanity: doing the same thing over and over again and expecting different results." – Albert Einstein

I'd started to see some of the signs; some of my patterns had become evident and I'd made a few decisions. In the winter prior to meeting John, I decided it was a good time to test out my new theory about "being open to love" – something I worked on in Step 3 (we'll explore that later). So, I placed an ad on a dating website and I was off to the races – or Starbucks, actually. I had several coffee dates with men who weren't remotely my type, but before long one came along who was intriguing, and I put my theory to the test. But before I share the story of The Fishmonger, let's clarify some of the criteria (characteristics and values) I was using to choose who would get a second date and who would not.

Characteristics Versus Values

It's difficult to break down the difference between day-to-day traits, or characteristics, and values. From my perspective you might really dig how someone is on a daily basis, but not jive at all with their values. Values are the guiding principles that you base your life on and your daily traits and characteristics are your behaviors or attributes. Here's an example: Say you meet someone who is really fun and adventurous. "Fun" and "adventurous" would be considered two of the person's characteristics. You also discover that being fun and adventurous for this person is accompanied by irresponsible behavior and little concern for financial security. If you value responsible behavior and financial security, then this person probably is not a good match for you. Knowing the difference between characteristics and values and being able to dig down deeply enough to discover a person's values is the point.

Sometimes the same words might go into both lists, you want someone who is adventurous (day to day), and someone who values spontaneity and adventure in their life. Going back to the example, you might also seek someone who values financial responsibility and security as well.

I'll share some ideas around values in the section before Exercise 3. And you'll have an opportunity to start your Characteristics list shortly. In the meantime, I discovered the subtle distinctions between characteristics and values the winter I was open to love.

Frog Story
THE FISHMONGER

The Fishmonger lived about an hour out of town, which wasn't usually appealing to me, but my motto meant I had to give him a chance. Our coffee date turned into a dinner and, before I knew it, a full-blown relationship. I was swept away in the current.

The Fishmonger had amazing blue eyes and a dimpled smile that could light up an entire restaurant. He was kind and extremely down to earth, the type of man you would see hanging off a boat in an Old Spice commercial – rugged and handsome. I had dated several "suits" and he was a breath of fresh air. He lived part time in a modern log cabin in the middle of the woods and owned a fish store right on the water.

A fish store? Say what?

Now, the "old me" would not have entertained the idea of dating a man who filleted fish for a living. That darn motto, however, meant I tried extra hard to stay open. It helped that when he looked at me with those big baby blues I felt absolutely cherished.

We were able to spend most weekends together because his store was closed a great deal in the winter. We adored each other. I loved his kids (a boy, 12, and a girl, 9) and his dog (a golden lab named Buddy) and we all got along really well. We spent most of the winter tucked away in that cabin cooking creative fish dinners and drinking wine in front of the stone fireplace. A few times we even got snowed in and couldn't get past the driveway for days. It was a heavenly place to get stranded. Things got serious relatively quickly.

Early in the spring, as the shop became busier, it became more evident that we wanted different things in life. The cabin was rented out, so we hung out in the apartment above his fish store. While I wanted to spend time out on the water or at the beach, he was busy working 12 or more hours a day. The fish store was his livelihood; I couldn't argue with that but a career change or retirement was nowhere in the plan.

The Fishmonger had characteristics that appealed to me. He was kind, funny, and quick to smile. But digging down to his core values, I discovered that we were not a match.

He would always be a man who lived off the land and wanted a simple life, while I preferred some of the more refined things in life. Don't get me wrong, I wasn't a spoiled princess, I just had dreams! He was content for the next 40 years to live above the fish store serving the people who lived in the beautiful houses on the lake, but I had a strong urge to live in one of those beautiful houses! Having a place on the lake was a big goal for me.

The Fishmonger and I had a wonderful winter, but, by summer, we both knew it wasn't going to go the distance. Our breakup was respectful and mature – one of the healthiest in my history. There was no drama, no yelling, just the quiet observation that we wanted different things from life. It hurt more because of the kids, but we agreed that breaking up was the right decision. And, we remained friends for quite a while afterwards.

The Fishmonger and I just didn't share the same vision for the future.

More important, the breakup left me open to meet John several months later.

Lessons from the Frog

We were right on the waterfront, close to where I wanted to be, but we weren't going to be doing any of the things I wanted to do together. To me the perfect day is spent at the beach, followed by a BBQ and a drink on the front porch and then maybe a bonfire.

The Fishmonger and I agreed that we didn't "fit" where our values and long-term goals came into play but this relationship was an excellent step in the right direction for me. I remained open and didn't take the first excuse for escape that came along (the long distance, his occupation, etc.). I also got some great experience having someone in my space – it had been so long since I'd dated anyone seriously that this was really important. And, it made me very aware of my own goal to be near the water. Having grown up in Nova Scotia, being by the water was a value that rose to the surface during this relationship – and I embraced it.

Giving off the strongest vibe to potential partners sometimes means (first) figuring out how to be happy and fulfilled without them!

So, shortly after breaking up with the Fishmonger, I decided to invest in my own small property near the lake (complete with a front porch and a fire pit). I was one step closer to creating the life I wanted. But you'll read more about this in my Summer of Fabulous.

Characteristics of Your Perfect Mate

We're not looking for people who are "perfect;" we're looking for the characteristics we want in a person who could be perfect for us.

The Fishmonger showed me that being with someone who didn't have a lifestyle I wanted forced me to become clearer on what I did want, and I discovered how important that lifestyle was to me. How did I want to spend my time? Did I want someone who traveled a lot? Or was a workaholic?

I needed to figure out what those characteristics would be. Remember: A clear vision is essential to creating the life you want.

Below are a few characteristics or personal traits I was looking for (this might help you start your list):

Funny	Successful	Intelligent
Kind	Able to relax	Great host
Generous	Adventurous	Helpful

Handsome   *Outdoorsy*   *Laid back*
Considerate   *Spontaneous*   *Family man*

Note: When you get to LEAP (Step 3), beware of people who are on their best dating behavior. They may be telling you things you want to hear!

When John came along, I reviewed the list and discovered he had nearly all my requirements. He even had some I hadn't thought of, like being able to fix almost anything. Bonus!

Had I not been clear with my list, I don't know if I would have recognized how perfect he was for me.

Whether you use lists or maps or pictures, think about what you are looking for and commit it to paper (or screen, fridge door, something). Then you can check it twice, like Jess did. Here's her story.

> *Had I not been clear, I don't know if I would have recognized how perfect he was for me.*

Success Story

JESS

Checking Your List

When I ended a rather challenging 14-year relationship in the summer of 2008, I had a good idea of what I felt was important to have in my next relationship.

My intention was to heal, rebuild my life and have fun. I asked a friend which dating website would be a good place to start. I chose one that required a 3-month financial commitment. In the fall of 2008, I went online for the first time to connect with other available women.

Within 3 months, I discovered that many of these women were in a similar situation to me. They were professional, career-oriented females who had recently come out of a long-term relationship; they were figuring out what they wanted and had a desire to connect with other women. Since we all seemed to be in a place of healing, I felt it was best to form a social group to develop these friendships and have some fun. Through this process, I became good friends with two of these women. Ironically, they became a couple.

As for dating, the first 9 months were disastrous. I was attracting emotionally unavailable women. It took me awhile to realize I was not emotionally available myself. I took a break from dating to regroup. I became clear about what was most important to me in a mate and mapped it out on a piece of paper, outlining what I felt were the most important characteristics. I then committed to a 100-day prosperity meditation. One of my requests centered around attracting an ideal mate. During this process, I chose to pull back from dating.

While in the final stretch of my prosperity meditation, I visited a free dating website. In order to view the women on this site, I was required to create a profile. Out of curiosity and without the intention of dating, I created a profile. Within two minutes of submitting it, I had two inquiries. I thought, "Wow! This is unexpected."

I followed up with both women. One was not a good fit right from our initial contact. The other I met a month after our initial email. I was in no rush to meet her, but within 4 weeks of our first meeting, we decided to date one another exclusively. Neither of us expected to meet someone online with whom we would be smitten.

When I went back to review my list, I was amazed at how most of the characteristics I had written down matched up so

well with this amazing woman. We have been together for 15
months and we're planning to live together next spring.

....

So Jess had her map and I had my list. What are the characteristics
you are looking for?

*Exercise 2**
. . . .
Characteristics of the Mate Perfect for You

Start your list with things that are important to you. If you really love travel,
for instance, you probably wouldn't want to hook up with a person who
never wants to go anywhere. If you're apt to spend money on fine dining
and wine, you should probably avoid someone who is a penny-pincher.

Think about past frogs. What did you like? What didn't you like? This
list will continue to evolve as you get clearer. Perhaps you would like to
put stars next to the deal breakers. If you want someone who has no
children, that might be a "*" item. Smoking, vegan, whatever you feel
is really important; don't feel shy about making it a deal breaker.

1. _____   6. _____

2. _____   7. _____

3. _____   8. _____

4. _____   9. _____

5. _____   10. _____

* Find this exercise on page 48 of *The Frog Whisperer Journal.*

What Are Your Values?

Values-based differences are difficult to overcome. Remember, values are the guiding principles for your life, things that define you and how you live. Some examples might be honesty, family, security. When one person values family and the other does not, you are going to fight about how you spend your time. When one person values freedom and the other values hard work, it might be a challenge.

You'll find values cropping up in various situations in your life outside of romantic relationships. If you have a co-worker who values hard work, while you value putting in your time and collecting your pay check, you may not be great friends with them. If you value honesty and integrity and your best friend is having an affair, you may have a very hard time not judging her behavior.

One of my values became really evident when I reconnected with a boy I'd known since Grade 4.

Frog Story
THE WOODSMAN

The Woodsman and I were officially boyfriend and girlfriend in sixth grade, in the Nova Scotia town where I grew up. When you are in grade six, it's never really official until someone writes it on the bathroom wall, so I wrote his name and drew a heart around it. He was shorter than me (not unusual at that age), cute, funny and very, very shy. We had about a 6-month relationship that involved holding hands, climbing trees and the odd kissing session. Frankly, he was more into the trees than he was into the kissing.

While I was living in Dallas many years later, The Woodsman and I reconnected on Classmates.com. He had become a craftsman of wood by trade, was divorced and was still short, cute, funny and shy. He lived a good, but quiet life in Halifax. We rekindled our relationship by computer and phone, and he came to visit me a few times. The relationship stalled after a few months as I started to realize we didn't share the same values.

One of the things I noticed right away was the different attitude he had toward money. I put it down to where he'd been raised. He'd grown up in Atlantic Canada (a part of Canada known for economic struggle), while I was living in Texas where abundance was plentiful. Dallas is a big wealthy oil town, whereas Halifax started as a fishing village so the mind-set was just different. It became clear to me that while I was focused on embracing wealth, he had no motivation towards it.

One of the final nails in The Woodsman's coffin was when we went out for a special New Year's Eve dinner. I had chosen the restaurant carefully so that it wouldn't be too expensive, but he was flabbergasted that a glass of wine cost $6. We have family jokes about my dad opening his wallet and moths flying out, so there was no way I was going to argue with someone about money for the rest of my life.

I exited that relationship quickly. I didn't tell The Woodsman the exact reason for my change of heart, and I feel bad that I left him high and dry like that. That's one frog I owe an apology.

Lessons from the Frog

There were many examples of our incompatibility, but one of our main differences was how we thought about and spent our money. I made a higher than average income and spent it with relative freedom. The Woodsman did okay financially, but reminded me of my dad when it came to spending. One of my goals in life was to attract prosperity and to never have to worry about paying the bills. The lesson from this frog brought that value to light for me. And it turns out it was a very important one to me!

When one of the leading causes of divorce is money, find out up front if you have similar goals and values when it comes to cash and spending.

If you tried to date someone who was a workaholic and you value free time to relax, you might be ready for the weekend at noon Friday and they won't finish working until 8 p.m.! No good. Or, like me and The Woodsman, you have an attitude of abundance while he is more apt to lean towards scarcity. You're setting yourself up for years of arguments over money. (And when the majority of relationships end because of money, this is a serious value to align.)

It's difficult to recognize someone who is perfect for you without having given it any thought ahead of time. As you see incompatibilities, bring them up and discuss them with your potential partner. Simply by recognizing them, you'll be able to talk them out and see if there is a solution.

Knowing what you value in your life is an important piece of finding the right person for you. When you chisel away the "trappings" of life – home, car, travel, etc. – what is it that really makes you happy? What are your big picture beliefs and ideas?

When you figure out what these are, the laws of attraction kick in, and your goal is to find someone who values the same things as you. You don't have to have all of your ideas and activities in common, but if you value the same things, you will have an easier time in your relationship.

Values Deal Breakers

Values matching is designed to help you attract your perfect mate. So how do you know when to throw in the towel? It's really hard to find two people who have the same ideas around money for instance. So if you find yourself dating someone who you are opposite from, ask yourself the question "Is this going to affect our future?" For the Woodsman and me, our value difference regarding money was definitely going to be a deal breaker. But maybe you're not as worried about it.

Most things can be negotiated. Consider all the famous couples made up of individuals with vastly different political views. I'd love to be a fly on the wall in James Carville and Mary Matalin's house – one's a democrat and one's a republican – what interesting dinner conversations they must have during an election!

John and I do not have the exact same principles when it comes to organization. His office always looks like a bomb went off and he'll spend much of his time in there searching for things. I, on the other hand, have systems to bring order to my office, and I know where everything is. This is not a major issue for us; it's minor. If he were a hoarder, for instance, we might have a much bigger problem.

> You don't have to have all of your ideas and activities in common, but if you value the same things, you will have an easier time in your relationship.

So think about the level of values mismatch and whether or not you can manage. There are many stories about people who are opposites figuring out how to make it work – it can be done. But if you care deeply for the same things that your partner does, it makes life easier.

And sometimes you know your values aren't in synch but the other person doesn't. That is a tough conversation to have – but have it you must. If your values don't match, you're wasting each other's time while each of you could both be moving on to someone more suited to you. In this example, Simon had to come clean.

Success Story

SIMON

Ego vs. Reality

After a rough divorce I was a really long time getting back on the dating bandwagon. I traveled a great deal for my consulting business and wasn't sure what type of woman would put up with so many days away from home.

I met Sara who was 29 and worked at a wellness center as a physiotherapist. She was attractive and sweet and made me feel great. But with 14 years between us, I was worried that she was too young for me. We dated on and off for several months, but eventually I had to tell her that it wasn't going to lead to anything long term.

We enjoyed each other's company, but really didn't have a lot in common and our values were a mismatch. While she loved going to the gym and hanging out at trendy restaurants, with my travel schedule I was more into relaxing at the movies or going for a bike ride. Restaurants were not a treat for me.

A few months after that difficult conversation with Sara, I met Andrea at a business conference. She was a consultant who was as busy as I was and it was refreshing to talk to a woman who really understood the challenges of my career. Although Sara was great for my ego, Andrea was more age appropriate, which came with many benefits. We were able to talk about work and life issues from a similar perspective and generation.

We're still in the early stages of our relationship and as we explore our interests, we find more and more common ground. Neither of us wants kids, which is a biggie. We enjoy the same movies and music and the more simple ways to relax after coming off the road. I'm not sure if this relationship will stand the test of time, but I can tell you I'm having a great time with Andrea and I'm going to enjoy every minute!

The laws of attraction and values matching actually apply to many things in life. Let's say you go to work for someone who is a big-time sales person, but they rarely tell the truth. If you value honesty, you will not be happy working for that person. Your values will get in the way.

I'll give you a few examples of my own values to help you create your list. Again you might put a star next to the most important values (like "honesty"):

I value…

Freedom	Animals	Beautiful
Honesty	Nature	surroundings
Travel	A beautiful view	Relaxation
Adventure	Lack of clutter	Hard work in
Spontaneity	Continuous	short periods
Entertaining	improvement	
Family	Knowledge	
Children	Earning money	

Do you see how values are different from the characteristics or traits you might look for in your perfect mate? Values are less personal and more big picture. Values are like your "theory on life."

Exercise 3*
● ● ● ● ● ● ● ● ● ● ●

What Values Will You and Your Perfect Mate Share?

Go back and review your perfect day with your perfect mate (Exercise 1). Then take a quick look at your list of characteristics from Exercise 2. Now back up a bit.

What are the broader values, the big-picture standards or ideals that would create this person?

1. _____	6. _____
2. _____	7. _____
3. _____	8. _____
4. _____	9. _____
5. _____	10. _____

When I was looking for my perfect mate I had to consider many of my values. I didn't want a workaholic, because I valued freedom. I didn't want someone with really small children, because I cherished travel, adventure and spontaneity. Although I love kids, raising them for 10-20 years is a big commitment.

Fortunately, or perhaps by design, John and I have many values that match. As I've said, we differ in a few areas, but none that are really crucial. What's great is that we both truly value family. When someone on either side of our family needs us, we are there as a team to help. In fact, when my step-daughter had a baby at 19 (whoops!), she and the baby moved in with us for a year. John and I were newly-weds and this could have been a rough year, but we both value family and it worked out well.

* Find this exercise on page 68 of *The Frog Whisperer Journal.*

And because John had older children when we met, we were able to blend as a family very easily. Having a grandson – who is now 4 and awesome – has given me the opportunity to be involved in a child's life from birth, while still maintaining all of the things that I treasure (like freedom and handing a child with poopy diapers back to the parent ☺).

What I really love about John is that he is willing to take time off work to travel. He loves to entertain just as much as I do. And he often says "yes" instead of "no" when I come up with even the most harebrained schemes. That's what keeps our lives spontaneous and I love it.

> *Values are like the glue that holds a relationship together.*

Asking the Right Questions

If you've ever asked yourself, "Why can't I find a good man?" you're not alone. I certainly have asked that question of myself many times. But a consultant friend once referenced an old saying that goes something like, "The measure of a person's success is directly related to the questions they ask themselves." Hmm, I pondered on that and realized that I was asking myself the wrong questions.

Rather than, "Why can't I find a good man?" I should have been asking, "Who do I need to become to attract the man who is perfect for me?" It wasn't about changing me, or being someone else, it was about being the best version of me. When I thought about that question over the course of a few weeks, I

> *Rather than, "Why can't I find a good man?" I should have been asking, "Who do I need to become to attract the man who is perfect for me?"*

realized I needed to become more open to love. I truly had been closed off.

You'd be surprised at the power of a good question. Rather than, "Why did this happen to me?" the question might be, "What's my lesson here?"

Instead of, "Why did he cheat on me?" a more empowering question might be, "How will I choose better next time?" Not being a victim in your "Why me?" questions is the first step to becoming the best version of yourself. Sometimes we need to let the question sit for awhile. That's okay. Your subconscious might just kick out an answer when you least expect it.

Being Happy

Have you ever really stopped to examine happiness? Are you aware of what truly makes you happy? Wikipedia says, "Happiness is a mental state of well-being characterized by positive emotions ranging from contentment to intense joy." Does happiness always produce the same level of joy? Probably not. I think we're looking for a balance of more joy and contentment than drama and negativity. No one is happy 100 percent of the time, at least no one that I know.

Perhaps part of our happiness stems from how we view life and its experiences. Do we stop and smell the roses, or do we barrel past them on the way to something else? I think there might be more exploring to be done around the area of noticing how you are in the world. Are you looking through a negative lens and missing joy? Or are you seeing beauty all around you?

Mary lives a quite untraditional life but it makes her happy.

Success Story

MARY

Houseless and Happy

Soon after my 28-year marriage ended I fell madly in love with a wonderful man. Although I was sure at the time he was my soul mate, the relationship ended abruptly. I was caught off guard, not only by his totally unexpected departure, but by how deeply grief stricken I became. It took over a year to heal my heart. I used to quip, "Now I understand what all those 'breaking up is hard to do' songs are all about!"

Two important things happened as a result of this love affair.

The searing pain of loss grew in me a greater capacity for compassion. I did not know you could physically hurt that bad and I became a kinder, gentler person. Second, I decided, "Enough drama already!" I set an intention for a new life: I wanted freedom, fun, adventure and passion.

Emptynested, single and able to work from anywhere, my life was a blank slate and I suddenly understood I could write a new exciting story. So I sold my dream house in 60 days, gave away most of my belongings to family and friends and paid off all debt. With money in the bank and a smile on my face I became "houseless and happy," living around the world without a plan, finding adventure after adventure and doing whatever good I could.

Because I am a speaker and consultant, my job allows me some flexibility. In the first five months I went to dozens of cities. One day I was a grape sorter in an Oregon vineyard. Other days found me surprising my mother with an endowed scholarship in her name for my alma mater, redecorating my friend's house in a week-long, around-the-clock session in what should have been a TV special, and dancing in a West Coast Swing flash mob at a mall. Presently I am house-sitting in Kauai for 3 months, with a daily practice of both sunrise Ashtanga yoga and sunset pupus (appetizers) and mai tais. Then I am off to the Netherlands and Germany for both business and pleasure. After that, who knows?

I suspect my prince will show up one day. In the meantime, my "new normal" involves love for my family and friends, work I am deeply passionate about, charming new people that I have the good fortune to meet, and adventures I never dreamed of. But of course, I did dream of these adventures when I set my intention to write a new story for my life. It is a juicy way to live.

· ·

It's funny, I consider myself to be someone who is pretty self-aware, but *The Happiness Project*, a book by Gretchen Rubin, got me really thinking differently about what makes me happy. And more importantly it made me think about how I could take responsibility for making myself happy. Some of Gretchen's ideas were simple reminders like "lighten up" and "take time for friends." The latter reinforced for me the importance of girlfriends and having someone with whom to share my ideas and fears.

I'll give you an example. This past Valentine's Day, my husband and I agreed to do cards only, but John gave me a surprise gift – a Scrabble game. I'd been playing Scrabble by myself on my iPad, for about 6 months, but I really craved playing with someone else.

This game made me really, really happy. Now I had somebody to challenge me and do battle with face to face. And through the hours a game may take, not only do we use our brains, but we also have a lot of laughs along the way. And I was even more thrilled that John (without my hinting or prodding) had come up with such a thoughtful gift. His gift, and my resulting happiness, got me exploring what types of things make me truly happy.

So what would it take to make you truly happy? I'll show you my list, so that you might get started on yours.

Happiness to me is:

- *Lying in bed on Sunday morning watching a movie or favorite TV show*
- *Playing a game (cards, board game, etc.) that promotes brain use*
- *Entertaining close friends (the more impromptu the better)*
- *Consuming great food, especially thai or sushi*
- *Witnessing something cool (like seeing a bald eagle fly by)*
- *Seeing a project come to life (like building our man cave last year)*
- *Sipping a glass of wine with my hubby on our porch*
- *Making money while I sleep*
- *Girlfriends sharing good food, wine and conversation*

That's my list. What would be on yours? Work through Exercise 4.

*Exercise 4**
What Would It Take to Make Me Truly Happy?

You may need to get a little introspective on this, but you can start with some easy ones. Start with Gretchen Rubin's reminders to lighten up and spend time with friends. Then you can start to go a little deeper. Don't worry. Be happy!

1. _____

2. _____

* Find this exercise on page 92 of *The Frog Whisperer Journal*.

3. _____

4. _____

5. _____

6. _____

7. _____

8. _____

9. _____

10. _____

Girl Power

We all know that friendships between women are special. "They shape who we are and who we are yet to be. They soothe our tumultuous inner world, fill the emotional gaps in our marriage, and help us remember who we really are." (Gale Berkowitz, 2002) A landmark UCLA study claims that men and women give off certain hormones while under stress and that women are actually capable of giving off more of the helpful hormone when tending to other women.

After reading more about this, I started thinking about my friendships. In my life before John, I don't really think I valued the female friends that I'd had. Because of this, some have gone by the wayside. Now, I find myself starting over, seeking new friendships. This past year I formed a book club with a group of my female neighbors. I also now meet regularly with other businesswomen.

I really enjoy it when John and I golf with other couples, because I'll often spend the entire day chatting with a woman about life. Last weekend we golfed with our neighbors, Tom and Bonnie. John and Tom talked about golf and travel, while Bonnie and I discussed a major illness she had just been diagnosed with. How two men can go 18 holes and not talk about anything of real significance is beyond me, but therein lies the difference!

I don't choose to be friends with a whole bunch of people, but I do consider the friendships I have to be rich and fulfilling.

What might you do to bring more happiness into your life through girlfriends? Here's one idea.

Exercise 5*
• • • • • • • • • • •
The Frog Whisperer Book Club

As I said, I've recently started a book club with some neighborhood women and we'll read any type of book. But if you're serious about find-ing lasting love, perhaps you'll form a club that will help support you?

Author's Note: I know I'm risking sounding self-promotional with this idea. (I think, as women, we shy away from this, but I'd encourage you to become a self-promoter!) And you know what? I really want you to help spread the word and create groups that will take finding love seriously. I want you to be so excited about the ideas in this book that you tell all of your single friends about it! And I also believe that the power of you as a group could be staggering.

So, what do you need to do?

Step 1. Seek out like-minded, positive women.

Step 2. Agree to meet on a regular basis. It doesn't have to be often; monthly or bi-monthly is fine.

Step 3. Perhaps you take turns hosting in your home or at a coffeehouse, whatever feels right. (Maybe a Starbucks that is located inside a bookstore?)

Step 4. Have your club members pick up a copy of *The Frog Whisperer* (and *Journal*).

* Find this exercise on page 139 of *The Frog Whisperer Journal.*

Step 5. During your meetings, have members share at least one positive thing that has changed since your last meeting and one thing that they are still working on. Be sure to tap into The Frog Whisperer Blog for additional support at www.frogwhisperer.com. Work very hard to keep the tone of your meetings positive. When someone is struggling, encourage them, but don't allow it to become a "bitch about men" club. Create the ground rules for a positive, healthy, supportive exchange within a group of fabulous women!

The Wounded

Wounds have a lot to do with the vibe we are putting out to the world.

Most everyone has been wounded to some degree. Our parents, no matter how great they are, have most likely left a mark. Past relationships, ouch. Even girlfriends can hurt us in ways we did not see coming. How many of us have scars from junior high or high school? *Oy vey!* There are many kinds of deep wounds – abuse, tragedy, loss, illness, heartache.

We've all got something.

Shaman Clay Miller says, "How you meet your losses will determine the amount of peace that you have." He helps people move past their wounds using his own brand of ancient wisdom. Whether we spend hours in therapy, scream into a canyon, or beat the trees with a Styrofoam pool noodle, there are many ways to try and heal our wounds. It goes right back to the old quote (no one knows who wrote this) "Life isn't about waiting for the storm to pass, it's about learning how to dance in the rain."

Life isn't about waiting for the storm to pass; it's about learning how to dance in the rain.

By taking responsibility for our wounds, we are taking charge of our own energy. I remember reading in Oprah's magazine that, when her show was on the air, she had a sign on the wall in her make-up room that read "Please be responsible for the energy that you bring into the room." I suspect her producers, prior to walking in and briefing her, would check themselves to see if they were bringing positive energy. And if not, make an adjustment.

Not letting our wounds and the fear created by those wounds define us and keep us from moving forward is the key. We need to recognize and treat our wounds. We also need to recognize the wounds of others and, as much as we might want to help, they really must treat their own wounds before moving on.

Story

SANDRA
Wounded, Bitterly Divorced

I know a woman named Sandra, who had been happily married for 10 years. She had two children, a big, beautiful house, cars, vacations, a successful husband and all of the trappings of wealth. But while Sandra was busy raising their children, her husband was busy finding a younger version of her. Her replacement. Ouch!

A long and bitter divorce left her struggling financially, getting back to work and hitting the wine more and more frequently. Her bitterness consumed her. Fast-forward 7 years, and Sandra is still stuck, still drinking too much and sometimes not very pleasant to be around. Her once bubbly, feisty personality has been consumed by the wound.

She got stuck in the wound and couldn't get out.

The Wound: The Badge of Honor

We sometimes carry around our wounds (our baggage) like badges of honor. In her book *Why People Don't Heal and How They Can,* Caroline Myss talks about "woundology." This is how we all come to the table carrying our wounds on our sleeve. When we first meet a person, we may hold those wounds out like a shield. By leading a conversation with "I was abused … I had a messy divorce … I was in a bad car accident," we are saying to the other person, "Beware, I'm damaged goods." Being wounded becomes our identity. Myss says choosing to stay stuck in woundology often comes at a terrible price: the loss of health.

When I was in the most emotionally unavailable place in my life, I would find any reason to pull the plug on a relationship.

As easy as it is to say "pick yourself up and brush yourself off," people need to heal in their own way. My point is not to take your wound lightly, but to make you aware of how you are presenting yourself to the outside world. Are you showing up as a victim? What are the results of staying bitter? Chances are, you will only be hurting yourself, like Sandra.

I've heard it said, "Most decisions based in fear are wrong." When I was in the most emotionally unavailable place in my life, I would find any reason to pull the plug on a relationship. A guy would call me a day late, and I would pull the chain and send him down the chute (into the "old boyfriend" pile). We'd have a fight, down the chute he'd go! If I didn't like his old beat-up car, down the chute!

Pushing guys away kept me safe. By not committing to anyone, I never had to deal with the pain of an actual, real-life relationship. Many of the excuses I found to leave a relationship were really my fear of commitment based on wounds that started when I was only 15 years old. While dating the Badass (who you'll read about in Step

2), a pivotal player in my life, I started building a safety wall around me. He made me fearful. Our relationship ended badly, and I surmised that all relationships meant pain. I made up my mind to never, ever cry like that over another man again. So, rather than get emotionally invested, I would send guys down the chute. Maybe you can relate to sabotaging a relationship like this?

Success Story

ELISA
Not Being Defined by the Wound

Thirtysomething Elisa was divorced with an 8-year-old daughter. A very attractive woman, she was just starting to get back onto the dating scene when tragedy struck.

Elisa was attacked and held hostage in her home at knifepoint by a deranged man from her neighborhood whom she did not know. Her daughter was locked away in a closet for over 12 hours while Elisa suffered violence and brutality. The ordeal ended in the early hours of the next morning when Elisa's attacker committed suicide.

This is the type of wound that could easily define someone. It could swallow a person whole and no one would blame the victim for sinking into a pit of despair. But Elisa was determined not to let this horrible attack ruin her life. She and her daughter sought counseling and over time she started to heal. A few years later she got married to a wonderful man who played a huge role in raising her daughter, who is now in her 20s. Although she has hit some bumps in the road, Elisa did not let her wound curb her entire life; she went on to thrive.

Perhaps Elisa's story will help provide you with hope that you, too, can move past a wound in your life.

Healing

Wounds can define us both positively or negatively. Getting past them is the only way to attract something more positive. If you have work to do, do it! And I'll say it many times: if therapy will get you there then please seek professional help.

Let's talk about some ways that you might move into a more positive space.

Talk to someone. Recently, I've been throwing hissy fits over silly little things, and I'm considering looking into therapy to figure out why I have a short fuse. When I lash out, I don't feel like myself. I don't want this behavior to continue. When John and I talked about what might be causing my meltdowns, I realized that it might be a result of some of the loss I have suffered.

Last year, my brother Cliff passed away very, very suddenly. He was only 53 years old (the same age as my husband) and the father of a 16-year-old. He was newly separated and had gone to Mexico to explore retirement places. He was in the beginning stages of realizing a dream he'd had for a very long time when an aneurysm interrupted his plans.

Telling my parents that their child had died was the worst day of my life. Although we all go about our days, dealing with our grief as individuals, Cliff's death has left a gaping hole in my life. Even though I feel tremendous support from John, I think an outsider might have some ideas that could help me move through it. Someone who is not so close to the family and situation might help me release my bottled-up emotions. So, if things don't improve, that may be my next step.

Take time out from the wound. Sometimes a short trip, or a change of venue can help us move from an upset or depressed state to something more positive. Maybe you hop on a plane and head to a sunny location. Or perhaps a more affordable option is a day trip out to the country. Fresh air has a way of shifting our perspective.

Perhaps you go for a walk and make a conscious decision to notice the flowers and the grass and the trees.

My friend Pat got divorced and moved to a new city to start her life over. She's making new friends (like me), ticking off things on her bucket list (like visiting the local provincial park and several of our most famous tourist spots), learning to Rollerblade, etc. Pat is reinventing herself and her new location is supporting that. Not everyone can pick up and move their life, but there might be an easier version of this that you can do.

On September 14, 2001, I had been holed up in my condo in Dallas for three solid days watching CNN. Like most of you, I couldn't pull myself away from the horror of the 9/11 tragedy. After being sent home from work in downtown Dallas for security reasons, I drove along Highway 75 looking up in the air thinking *Is a plane going to crash near here?* It was such madness. I sat in front of the TV crying for nearly 12 hours, and finally I had to change venues. I put on my yoga pants and sneakers, and I headed out to the lake. Instantly, I felt different. My tears dried up, and I started to stand up tall again. I noticed the birds, the flowers, the trees, and it seemed like life might just go on. I realize this is just my little microcosmic view of this massive tragedy, so please don't think I'm minimizing it.

Exercise 6*
• • • • • • • • • • •

Get to the Heart of the Wound

Take out your journal or a piece of paper. Make a list with two columns. Label the first column "Wound" and label the second column "This Made Me Feel…"

List your wounds and start writing down all of the feelings that come to you as a result of each wound.

* Find this exercise on page 163 of *The Frog Whisperer Journal.*

Here's my own example, with just a few of my wounds:

Wound	This Made Me Feel...
The Badass – Breaks my Heart	Stupid, unlovable, naïve, taken advantage of, abandoned by friends, lonely
Dad gets laid off (depression), brothers leave home.	Abandoned, lonely, sad, worried
The Suit – didn't choose me	Why am I not good enough?
My brother dies	Alone (without advice), worried (about Alex (niece), my family), gaping hole, sad, depressed, angry "it's not fair," etc.

I realize these ideas are pretty basic, but if you can't afford years of therapy, maybe there is some value here for you.

And speaking of seeking help ... For many people, I realize there is more at stake. You may suffer from mental illness or a chemical imbalance that doesn't make healing easy. Please know that I don't take something like this lightly. Please check in with your professional before taking any action. I'm coming to you as a reporter on love, not as a therapist.

Frog Story
THE HOT DIVORCÉ

While living in Dallas, I worked with a fellow named Joe who had a brother-in-law who was going through a painful divorce. His name was Ben and he had a brilliant big smile and piercing blue eyes. He was a young hottie. Joe suggested that Ben and I get together after he had introduced us at a party and Ben had expressed some interest in me.

Ben was only a few months into his divorce and I was quite nervous about getting hooked up with him. But he was cute and wounded and I felt like I could help him – let's just say my Florence Nightingale archetype took over and common sense went out the window.

We started dating and it was so much fun. I knew he was in pain, but he smiled so much when we were together that it just made me happy. We got close very quickly and spent a lot of time together over several months. We had some great dinners, picnics in the park and a lot of romantic evenings with just the two of us. We had created a little world in a bubble.

But the reality of his emotional healing started to kick in when we'd get into fights. We'd be arguing about something that had absolutely nothing to do with our relationship and I realized he was arguing with his ex-wife. She had walked out on him without a lot of explanation and he had felt like he didn't have any closure. He had never gotten to express himself or his feelings about the failure of the relationship so there were a lot of pent-up emotions there.

I had to break off the relationship out of self-preservation but I was so sad. We really cared a lot about each other. The timing was just wrong.

Lessons from the Frog

I probably helped Ben start to get his mojo back (more on Mojo in Step 2), but being the rebound girl sucked. I was falling head over heels with this guy and although he loved our time together, he was emotionally unavailable. What I learned was that I needed to be very careful about getting into relationships with people who were not yet healed. It was not my job to help people get their mojo back.

Be very careful about getting into relationships with people who are not yet healed. It's not your job to help them get their mojo back.

Saving the Wounded

Sometimes we're not the one who is wounded.

But what do we do when we meet someone who is? Do we try to help them? Or do we assess where they are in their recovery and be aware? I learned the lesson that I am not responsible for another person's path in life. I could not heal Ben. I was a nice distraction for him, but he wasn't ready for what I wanted, not even close. The Hot Divorcé was a painful lesson, but I later would recognize the walking wounded more quickly and would not embroil myself.

When I look back, I realize that Ben was a safe choice for me because I was emotionally unavailable at that time too. I think that he was the reason I started to recognize the pattern – first The Badass then The Suit (more on these Frogs later). But even though I recognized it, I still didn't make a change until I was really ready to settle down, which would be years later. I hope I can help save you some time and heartache.

Many of you have been in this place before when you knew someone wasn't ready. Or maybe you've even been involved with someone who was still married? Yikes – talk about being emotionally unavailable. I want you to really see that when you choose people who are not available – i.e., newly divorced or still married – you are choosing people who may be safe for you, where there is little chance for commitment.

Of course there are exceptions to the rule. You fall in love with someone who is just leaving a marriage and you end up together. I think that's happening more now than before. Years ago, married couples rarely divorced. But I think times are changing and people don't want to stay years in a marriage that doesn't work.

> *When you are truly serious about finding love, these people (the highly wounded, the married) will not even enter your radar.*

Terri and Chris were such an exception but it took them a long time to recognize it – they just weren't READY.

Success Story

TERRI

When Waiting Pays Off

I met Chris the spring of 2005 and we automatically hit it off as friends with a strong mutual respect for each other. The sexual chemistry was there too, but we were both married and respected each other's situations. I was in the last trimester, so to speak, of an 18-year marriage and loved my husband as a friend but not as a lover. He was a wonderful provider, father and supporter, but did nothing for me as a woman. During my marriage, I put my children's needs first and gave them 110% of my energy.

I ultimately separated from my husband in the fall of that year. Chris had nothing to do with the demise of the marriage, as it was already broken when we met and I certainly didn't leave my husband to be with him.

Over the next few months, Chris and I became very close. We had similar interests and became confidantes for each other. Because he was still married, we decided to be just good friends. We would meet once or twice a week, have coffee, go for a run, ride our bicycles or simply sit in the gardens and admire the flowers. We were like carbon copies of each other; we had all the same interests. Our friendship continued for another 18 months before he finally ended his marriage. I was initially quite excited that he finally left her, as in my mind we could now be together. He, however, had a different vision. He didn't want to be involved with anybody. He had been in an awful marriage and wanted to be free and uncommitted to anyone.

By this time, I had started to see another person, as I was tired of waiting for Chris to come around. All the while, we still continued to meet twice a week, talk on the phone and pour our hearts out to each other. I would get excited when we spoke and sent text messages daily and we'd meet each week. I would tell him my horror stories with my boyfriend and he would tell me his and we would help each other resolve the issues of the day. One day after years of being friends we were having our usual coffee get together, and he said, "You really love me, don't you?"

"Yes," I said. "I do." And we've never looked back.

That was in April of 2009. We joke about finally being together and wonder what life will be like after the "honeymoon" phase – it hasn't ended yet. All our friends said, "It's about time you two finally announced it." I guess we weren't hiding it too well.

The fact that we were best friends before committing to each other in an intimate relationship sealed it all for us. We have such a natural and loving relationship and I finally feel like I am a woman.

I have found my true love.

Divorce: The Big Wound

Although I haven't experienced it, divorce is a common – and gigantic – wound. I believe it's the closest thing to having someone you love die. Because really, your dreams die when a divorce occurs. No matter who initiates the divorce, there's going to be pain. And when you are the one who wants to stay in the marriage and keep the family together, your pain will be amplified. Sometimes you might still love the person you are divorcing, but you just can't live the same way anymore. You need to break free and find yourself. You need a fresh start. And what must make it even more difficult is moving from a two-parent situation to single parent. I can't imagine having to make that choice. And frankly, I think that's why so many people stay married longer than they should – it's just so much for one person to juggle physically, emotionally, and especially financially. It takes guts to walk away.

Someone who is betrayed might take much longer to heal than someone who leaves a marriage due to lack of love. There's no recipe, but perhaps finding people with common heartache to talk to can help. It's become so normal for people to lose themselves in a marriage and as parents that it's no wonder some choose to leave the marriage in search of themselves.

But divorce does not mean that your life is over. It means that you have to create a new normal for yourself. Where you had a partner to help with finances, decisions, child-rearing, and household chores, you may now be on your own. No matter how the situation unfolds, it's never going to be a piece of cake, even if you're the one seeking the change. But there is some hope. After some time, you'll be able to manage your new life and experience love again. Coming back after a divorce is difficult, but as Stuart shows us, it is possible!

Success Story

STUART

Picking Yourself Up Off the Floor

I was completely blindsided when my beautiful wife of 20 years told me that she wanted a divorce. She was going through a mid-life crisis of sorts. She had lost a parent, lost a career and our son had grown up and no longer needed her in the same way. Her identity had become lost in her roles of daughter, mother and wife and she wanted out so that she could find herself.

I was devastated. I didn't want a divorce. I loved her and I wanted to keep my family together. I was in denial for the first few months and in utter misery. My business had been thriving, which meant a lot of travel and speeches. I'd stand up on stage in the middle of this crisis thinking, "There's no way I can pull this off." But somehow I got through it. I think sometimes I got even better responses because of the vulnerability I was showing the audience. The nights on the road were the worst. I had nightmares almost constantly and the lack of sleep was taking its toll. My weight was dropping and my friends were getting worried.

I finally accepted the fact that I could not control this situation. I was willing to do anything to make it work, but she wanted out. So I agreed and we moved forward with the separation and divorce. To me it felt as though someone had died, and I had never experienced this type of pain in my life.

About a year later, I started to see the light at the end of the tunnel. I started to feel human again. That was when I met Lisa. We met at a business event that was several days long and after the third day, I started to think, "Maybe there is life after divorce."

She was beautiful and talented and was really into me. We shared a lot of the same interests and both treasured food and music. I was really unsure whether or not I should move ahead with this relationship, but over time I asked her all of the important questions I wanted answers to. I asked her about religion, money, travel, long-term goals, children, etc., and I loved everything she said. I thought the questions would scare her away, but nope. And it turned out, we were compatible.

It's been over a year and Lisa and I are doing great. The previous year was hell, but I made it through and came out at the other end with new love and a new attitude about life. You see, you don't really realize how precious each "high" moment is until you've lived the "lows." Now, I don't take them for granted.

••

Now I know Stuart's story (he and Lisa are now happily married, by the way) is one that many people can relate to. No matter which side you are on, divorce can leave you feeling weak and vulnerable. And that's why taking your time after divorce and allowing yourself to heal is important. Even if there is a feeling of relief in the early stages of breakup, chances are you could still go through some, if not all, of the phases of grief.

Elisabeth Kübler-Ross first introduced the five stages of grief in her book *On Death and Dying* but they relate well to any form of tragedy. Stuart, for instance, had to move through all of these stages before he could see any signs of hope.

The stages are:

- Denial: "This can't be happening."
- Anger: "It's not fair; how dare you not love me anymore."
- Bargaining: "Let's just try to make it work."
- Depression: "I'm so sad, why bother with anything?"

• Acceptance: "It's going to be OK."

Now, everybody has to go through things differently. Stuart got his mojo back partly by experiencing the feelings and allowing the time to pass. He didn't start dating a month after being separated. He waited quite a long time before entertaining the idea. You might think that Lisa helped him get his mojo back, and she probably did. But Stuart put a lot of hours into therapy to help move him through the emotions of his divorce before he could move into a positive, healthy relationship.

Ideas to Ponder

Not allowing your wounds to become your identity is a powerful piece of this lesson, but moving past them to design your perfect life is key. And for goodness' sake, if you need professional help, go get it! There are counselors, coaches, therapists, support groups, psychiatrists, psychologists, and healers for just about every issue you can imagine. Not every method or individual might be for you. If someone doesn't work, move on to someone else. And be aware that there are rarely quick fixes to healing. Dr. Phil always says, "You cannot change what you don't acknowledge" so if you are in pain and need help, for heavens' sake acknowledge it and seek help.

Even if you aren't wounded here are a few ideas to help you gain some clarity.

• What would a perfect day in your life look like in 5 years? Write it down in your *Frog Whisperer Journal* and review it frequently.

• What are the characteristics of your perfect mate?

• What do you value in your life?

- What are your wounds? (Make a list and we'll work more on this in Step 2.) What are you doing to help you move past them?

Are You Ready?

I believe finding true love comes down to readiness. I paid lip service to being ready for many years before I actually *was* ready to find love. I was fooling myself, because I hadn't really done any of the work. I didn't know what I was looking for or what I valued. And I had no idea what was holding me back.

Exercise 7*

Are You Ready to Be in the Dating/ Relationship Game?

Here's a quick quiz to help you determine if you are ready to proceed to Step 2: SET.

1. Are you happy with yourself?
   (Or are you miserable because you've put on 50 pounds since your divorce?)

2. Are you looking for someone to rescue you or take care of you?
   (If you answered "yes" to this one, you may not be ready.)

3. Is there room in your life for a relationship?
   (Or do you have three kids and work a 60-hour week?)

4. Has enough time passed since your last relationship?
   (Or are you still wounded?)

* Find this exercise on page 189 of *The Frog Whisperer Journal.*

5. Is your emotional baggage cleared up?
   (Have you forgiven and forgotten all the crap from your past?)

6. Are you financially sound?
   (Or are you hoping someone will come along and save you?)

7. Are you 100% committed to finding true love?
   (Or are you just dating for fun? There's no harm in that, by the way!)

8. Are you truly open to love?

If you've answered "no" to 3 or more of these questions, then you still may have more work to do. If not, then carry on.

Now that you've established that you're ready, what you want in your life, and the type of partner that might fit into your perfect situation, you're ready to move on to Step 2: SET.

STEP 2 – SET

What's Needed to Get There?

"Your task is not to seek for love, but merely to seek and find all the barriers within yourself that you have built against it."

Rumi

Now that we've identified your readiness to get into a relationship, we're going to discuss your ideas around love, what might help you get in the game, and how to get your mojo back. It's not about being fake, or insincere; being the most fabulous version of yourself is the goal. If you want to attract that perfect person, it's essential that you know what makes you happy and take steps to get there.

Step 2: SET has two parts to it – getting your psyche (your spirit) set and then setting the stage. That is, doing the work on the inside and then preparing yourself and your environment to LEAP.

I like to think of this first part of SET as the "get happy process." Now, this makes it sound easy and fun. It's not likely to be. Getting

It's not about being fake, or insincere; being the most fabulous version of yourself is the goal.

happy will take some introspection; you'll need to take a long, hard look at yourself and be honest.

I'll make some suggestions and offer some techniques. At this stage in the process you might find you need to seek counsel. You may just need someone objective to act as a sounding board or you may have deep wounds that require more work.

Once your psyche is SET, it will be time to prepare your surroundings – your whole environment and vibe need to be open to letting someone else be welcome.

Your Ideas/Perceptions about Love

It's interesting to analyze how you feel about love. What does it mean to you? At one point in my late 20s I thought love meant less freedom, i.e., if I got married, I'd have to have children and that would mean I would never travel or do anything fun again.

In my late 30s, after a few painful breakups, I thought love equaled pain.

By finding a few role models, and seeing the types of relationships they had, I realized I could have exactly what I wanted from a loving relationship, and on my terms. I didn't need to be "someone's wife," I could still be me and keep all of the freedom I so treasured!

What are some of the things that you equate with love and where did you get them? Our parents sometimes have influence over this area, especially if they ended their marriage or there was infidelity that tore the family apart. Have you taken on ideas about relationships from the media or movies? When you discover what has helped you form your ideas about love, sometimes that makes it easier to identify and reformat.

Our brains have the ability to hold on to pieces of information. For instance, we have tapes running constantly in our brains about how we should be in the world, based on things our parents said to us or things we picked up over time. Heck, just comparing yourself to stars in magazines could do in your mojo and make you think you were old, fat and ugly.

Negative tapes might have a big impact on our lives. We might tell ourselves "My butt is huge; I'm not pretty enough; I'm not worthy." Where did that noise come from? So when it comes time to fall in love, those tapes could make us think we really don't deserve love.

So how do we erase those negative tapes and focus on the positive aspects of ourselves? How do we re-program our outcomes? We'll talk about some techniques later in this chapter under the heading "Love Mantras," but basically, we can start to run our own tapes using language that we design. "I am a smart, attractive, and powerful woman" might be something you say to yourself every day.

This kind of makes me laugh because *Saturday Night Live* had a sketch years ago featuring mock self-help show host Stuart Smalley. I know if you saw Stuart saying things like "I'm good enough, I'm smart enough, and gosh darn it people like me" you might think running a positive tape is stupid. But you've got to look at the science. Your brain doesn't know what's true and what's not true. And I believe if you tell yourself you're fabulous often enough, you'll step into it.

Once you establish your ideas about love, and rectify anything that might be blocking you, you'll then be ready to move forward into the next step. Unless, of course, you're already involved or stuck.

For additional help with this, check out *The Frog Whisperer Positive Practice Audio.*

Are You Already Involved?

If you find yourself currently in a situation that keeps you emotionally unavailable, you must acknowledge it before you can change anything. If you're hung up on an ex-boyfriend, still married or still involved with someone, you have to get your ducks in a row before moving toward love. The first step is acknowledging what's in your way. If you're healing from a wound, perhaps you need some time? Or if it's someone from your past who's holding you up, maybe you need to get some closure through one last phone call or a letter. Perhaps you're simply too busy and you need to free up some time and space in your life for a relationship.

If you are in a marriage that is over in your mind, but you are not yet out of it, then get out first! You need to be physically and emotionally available before even starting to think about dating again.

What if You're Just Stuck?

My friend Kara, a beautiful, 48-year-old nurse, is a great example of someone who was stuck. She thought Rick, a handsome firefighter, was her soul mate, but they struggled to keep their relationship together for any length of time. Trust issues and baggage would get in the way and they would end up apart again.

For nearly 10 years they were on and off. They would break up and Kara would try to see other men, always with Rick in the back of her mind. Rarely, would it ever work out, because Kara was stuck.

But a new day has dawned for Kara. She has ended her relationship with Rick for the very last time and is 100% committed to moving forward with her life. She's taking classes and attending events that will allow her to evolve as a person. She's really working hard to unload her baggage and get happy prior to putting herself out there on the dating scene.

Kara is doing everything to move in a positive direction and when she's truly ready, she'll open up to being available for Mr. Right.

To recognize if you're stuck, you might ask yourself "Am I repeating the same patterns?" "Am I in a rut?" "Have I wanted something for years that I just can't seem to achieve?" I can certainly relate to this last one, and it wasn't until I took some conscious action that I became unstuck. The danger of being stuck and remaining there for years is that you'll live your life on half throttle. I know this from experience. When I look back at how many years I played it small and safe, I get sad for the person that was me.

How High Are Your Walls?

Some of us build the walls around us so high that no one could ever scale them. They protect us. They keep people out and, most importantly, they keep us out of danger of getting hurt in relationships. We build them out of necessity but the irony is that if we want to truly live, they must come down.

I had built the equivalent of Mt. Everest around me, keeping love safely out! I think one of my recurring mistakes in my dating life was playing Jane Seinfeld. I would wait to find something wrong with the person so that I could break it off. That kept me safe in my emotional cocoon, gigantic walls intact. Kind of like Jerry and Elaine on *Seinfeld*. They always had the most ridiculous reasons for breaking up with someone – their hands were too big (man hands), their voice was too soft (low talker). They were practiced commitment-phobes! It was funny, but sad and when my friends starting calling me Jane Seinfeld, I took the hint!

We often think that it's mostly men who are commitment-phobes and emotionally unavailable. I'm not sure why that is. Obviously Elaine and Jerry were; you'll see later that I was with The Suit; and Margaret definitely was. Perhaps it's just harder to recognize in ourselves. Margaret certainly took a long time to see her patterns.

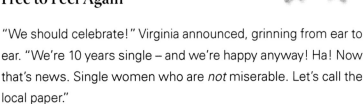

Success Story

MARGARET

Free to Feel Again

"We should celebrate!" Virginia announced, grinning from ear to ear. "We're 10 years single – and we're happy anyway! Ha! Now that's news. Single women who are *not* miserable. Let's call the local paper."

We laughed, feeling quite content with ourselves. After all, we had proven all the stereotypes wrong! Sure, we were single ladies in our 50s, but we certainly weren't spinsters – far from it, in fact! We were accomplished modern women, with grown children and grandkids, homes of our own, businesses to run and active, healthy lifestyles. We really didn't *need* a man to make our worlds turn. We were doing just fine, thank you very much.

Mmm-hmm. *Ri-i-ight.* Try telling that to my mother.

"Margaret, now you listen to me. You need to find someone! Stop picking holes with everyone you date!"

"Mom, I *am* happy!" I insisted. "Really, I am. I'm just not looking for anything serious right now."

(Was that an echo? I must have heard myself say that a hundred times – and when I said it to my closest friends, I also confessed, "I just want hot sex!")

Underneath my "happy single lady" persona, I was deeply in love with falling in love. The adrenaline of a first date, the anticipation of his returning text, the thrill of a first kiss … it was thoroughly intoxicating, and I was happily drunk on every drop of it.

And, like any good drunk, this was my not-so-secret hiding spot.

Truth be told, I had come to see myself as a "runner" – and everyone else had too. Over the decade since my divorce, I had dated plenty of eligible bachelors. But my pattern never failed to surface: the relationship would progress, things would get serious, and suddenly a field of flaws would appear before my eyes. *He was rude with the taxi driver; he doesn't exercise; he wears weird socks* ... all surmountable things, really. And yet, these details got under my skin ... and they snowballed... and before either one of us knew what was happening, I would be out the door. Again. *(Sigh)*

It was a series of seemingly unrelated events that finally unraveled my pattern, and it started on the day a colleague said to me, "Margaret, you must get asked out a lot."

I raised my eyebrows and shook my head, but she persisted. "Not even the smart, business types?"

I shrugged her off. "Not really – and I'm glad about that! I have no desire to clean house and cook for another man."

She looked a little surprised by my comment. "But, don't you want a man to change the oil in your car and fix the water heater when it breaks? I mean, for all that we do for them, they certainly bring us plenty in return."

Perhaps it was her matter-of-fact tone that stopped me in my tracks. Maybe it was the simple truth of her comment? Suddenly I had a stark realization: I had a completely one-sided view of partnership! All I had seen was the support that women contributed!

Wow! I was deeply shocked to come face-to-face with my own limiting beliefs. How could I be so blind to the valuable contribution of the masculine side of the equation?

A little piece of my armor started to crumble.

Weeks later, I found myself sitting with a hypnotherapist who asked me to provide word associations for some common, everyday words. "What do these things mean to you?"

House ... Home ... Husband ... Wife... Marriage ...

Imagine my surprise when I saw myself write "boredom" next to the word *marriage*.

Hmm, *very interesting!* No wonder I was single! Another piece of my armor had been revealed.

Several months later, at a personal growth event, I listened intently as the presenter told the crowd, "If you're not in a relationship, you need to ask yourself what you're afraid of."

"Well, that's stupid," I thought. "I am perfectly happy as a single woman."

Try as I might to dismiss his comments, they continued to haunt me for weeks. It was at least a month before I finally sat myself down, journal in hand, to ask: What am I afraid of?

It didn't take long to get to my basic truth: "I am afraid of loving someone so deeply that I could end up hurt again." It was as simple as that.

Clink Another piece of my armor dropped away.

At the urging of a friend, I decided to take the plunge into online dating. Within days of setting up my profile, I was communicating with a dozen eligible bachelors. Two seemed especially interesting, and one of them lived nearby, so we met for coffee. To my great surprise and delight, we seemed to click instantly!

On the way home, I called my daughter. "This is a really special guy! Now I don't even want to meet the other one."

"Mom," she cautioned, "just be open to meeting him. You never know where it will lead."

She's right, I thought. I should stay open to possibilities.

Clunk More armor fell.

The second gentleman, Peter, caught my eye with an exceptionally witty profile. I noticed we had a lot in common, and his closing line made me smile.

He lived quite a distance from me, so we decided to talk by phone for awhile. I found him to be warm and engaging, and funny, with a deep, resonant voice that made my knees weak.

One call led to the next, each call longer than the last, and I found myself really enjoying him! One night we talked and laughed together for six hours straight! He was so much fun.

And yet, after 40+ hours of connecting by phone, we still hadn't met. Naturally, concerns crept in. *This has been so perfect – and I don't even know what he looks like! If we meet, it might be awful!* In a wave of discomfort, I could feel myself reaching for my armor – and finding precious little of it left. I suddenly felt naked. *What am I doing?*

With a few deep breaths and a little pep talk, I got through it.

On the day we planned to meet, a snowstorm came in and his flight was canceled. Undeterred, he arrived by ferry four hours later. There I stood, waiting for him in the blowing snow. We made eye contact, and without a word he pulled me into his arms for a deep, magical, heartfelt kiss. Every last concern I had just melted away in that moment … and the last of my armor did too.

The months since then have been so exciting! Having released the need to protect myself and be in control, I'm discovering and exploring and feeling – and I'm loving every bit of it. To experience this relationship without a suit of armor is such a wonderful thrill! I feel so young and alive, full of laughter and joy.

This journey is still unfolding, and I still have so much to learn … but at least now, I can say, "Look Ma, no running!"

· ·

Did Margaret have some views about the roles in marriage that perhaps you can identify with? I believe roles (who does what) are something that can be negotiated. Remember you're designing *your* perfect life.

Aside from that, it took Margaret awhile to see that she'd been emotionally unavailable. It's a lot easier to identify in someone else – although that can take some time too. Here's another example of my own journey, this time with The Suit.

Frog Story
THE SUIT

The Suit came along when I had just arrived home from Australia.

I had traveled for a year in the South Pacific – a year that may have been one of the best of my life. I was 25 years old when I lived in Australia; I looked good, felt good and I felt healthy. I worked out regularly when I wasn't traveling. I ate a lot of fish, veggies and rice (the Asian influence). And although I had traveled to Australia on my own, once I landed in Oz, I rarely felt lonely (a first in my life).

Based out of Sydney, my phone rang more often that year than ever before. I made friends through my work and dated frequently. Several people took me under their wings and made sure I had a true Australian experience, complete with trips to the horse races, the outback and the Great Barrier Reef. I ended up traveling the entire perimeter of that continent and spent a great deal of time working on both a fishing trawler and a cruise ship. I soaked it up and probably saw more of that country than the majority of native Aussies. I felt fabulously empowered, like I was drinking in everything life had to offer.

When I came back from Australia I was a different person. I was happy and had more confidence. About a year after I returned, I met The Suit. I was working at a radio station as an administrative assistant, temping for a woman who had gone on maternity leave. She wasn't a real firecracker, so everything I did that was remotely clever was met with enthusiasm by the sales team I supported. It didn't hurt that I was 25 and cute.

The Suit worked for the competing radio station. (My boss freaked out about me "sleeping with the enemy.") When I first laid eyes on him, I saw a good-looking, very self-assured man with a chiseled face. He had a big personality and the designer suit and tie to match. He was of average height, but I saw him as tall. He looked every bit the part of the advertising sales executive. I was completely taken by him as he was by me.

We dated for 4 years and had a blast. We ate at the best restaurants, sometimes arriving in limos (radio station perks), went to concerts and traveled. We laughed a lot. I transitioned into a new job working for a motivational speaker and she took one look in my eyes and saw this amazing light. She saw that I was in love – hook, line and sinker. The red roses came into the office by the dozens; I had found the man I was going to marry.

At least that's what I thought!

Around year four, I started to realize our relationship wasn't moving forward. I spent a lot of time at The Suit's place, but he had never asked me to move in. In fact, we rarely talked about our future together. When we traveled it was always business related so we were never alone. Rarely, did we take a trip with just the two of us. In fact, I took a 3-week trip to Europe by myself because I was tired of waiting for him to travel with me.

The Suit was emotionally unavailable to me. I remembered the way he had once looked at me – I didn't see that look in his eyes anymore. And my eyes were starting to cloud over as well.

The final straw came when The Suit put in an offer on a new house without even factoring me into the equation. Ouch! One morning I woke up with clarity: this relationship was going nowhere. I was finished.

Our breakup was rough on both of us. He thought there was someone else, but that was not true. We still loved each other, but we knew it wasn't working. Several months after the breakup he called and wanted to get together.

Even though I had been recruited to work in Vancouver and was getting ready to move, I agreed to see him this one last time. This was his last shot at trying to keep me. He took me to a beautiful Japanese restaurant for dinner and popped open a jewelry box that held … a watch! A watch?

I should have said, "Dude, where's the ring?" but didn't. Was a watch supposed to turn the tides and make me want to stay? Too little, too late. The Suit was not capable of commitment, even on the smallest levels. I moved away and started to heal.

Ironically, one of my Christmas gifts to him had been a weekend workshop on forgiveness. Because I broke up with him, I figured I would be the subject of his anger that weekend. It turned out he had all kinds of family issues that needed clearing. Funny enough, once this was done, The Suit was actually freed up to fall in love. He was married within a couple of years and has since had a couple of kids. You're welcome, Mr. Suit!

Lessons from the Frog

I don't consider The Suit a waste of time. He showed me what "emotionally unavailable" looked like. In fact, I came to realize later that I was the one who was unavailable and that's why I attracted men like him. They kept me safe.

You'd think I would have been bitter about The Suit. Being "the one before the one and only" kind of sucked. But I realized that marrying him and settling down in my hometown was not in the cards for me. I was meant for different things – I was meant to have a big career, move to Vancouver and then Dallas. It would have been much different had I stayed.

I think The Suit knew that he could not have made me happy and was protecting himself by not proposing. Marriage and babies in my 30s was not in the cards for me, and I was totally cool with this situation once I healed.

I was meant to find real love. Love that I didn't have to fight for. Love that I didn't have to jump up and down and say, "Pay attention to me! Love me!" The big lesson from The Suit: I never once told him what I wanted; I never told him my goals or when I was angry or disappointed. There were many times I cried myself silently to sleep. He always put me last because I didn't demand more from him. Over time I lost myself; my self-esteem started to seep away, and I let it happen. Big, big lesson.

One thing that popped up occasionally when The Suit and I were dating was how I was treated as his girlfriend. His company was nice to include girlfriends on some events, but there were others when it was spouses only. I started to think about what it meant to be married and ultimately I felt that you were taken more seriously if you walked down the aisle.

You may have your own ideas about marriage, and I think everyone has to do what is right for them, but for me, I knew that I wanted to be married. I feel great when I hear John say "my wife" and my belief is that the outside world takes our relationship more seriously. Certainly there are people who have success without marriage – we have several friends who have never married and we barely know it. They call each other husband and wife, so we just don't know the difference. There are certainly arguments in both directions. You decide.

Where'd Your Mojo Go?

Your mojo is your self-esteem – your chutzpah, the bravado that you take to the world that says, "I'm fabulous!" It comes in waves. Sometimes you feel like you are invincible, that everything is going your way, and sometimes you're mopping the floor with your mojo, it's simply gone. Like most things in this book, acknowledging where your mojo is at is the first step.

There have been a number of frogs in my life that have affected my mojo. Perhaps you can relate? The Suit obviously had an effect. I moved out to Vancouver afterwards to "lick my wounds" and had a very hard time getting back in the dating pond. I probably went a year without dating anyone, but really didn't let anyone in for several years after that.

Why? Because I didn't feel fabulous. My self-esteem was low. My mojo was nowhere to be found! Even though I had broken up with The Suit, I still felt hurt that I was someone not worthy of the happy ending. I allowed the fact that he hopped into a relationship with someone else so quickly to really undermine my mojo. And, the fact that I just wasn't "the one" for him helped that along.

You Complete Me – Ugh!

Remember how Tom Cruise swoops in on Renée Zellweger in *Jerry Maguire* with the line "you complete me?" From a self-esteem perspective, this sounds like a lot of bunk! Being whole is the best way to enter a relationship.

In Neale Donald Walsch's book, *Conversations with God*, he says, "It's very romantic to say that you were 'nothing' until that special other came along, but it's not true. Worse, it puts an incredible pressure on the other to be all sorts of things he or she is not. Not wanting to 'let you down,' they try very hard to be and do these things until they cannot anymore. They can no longer complete your picture of them. They can no longer fill the roles to which they have been assigned. Resentment builds. Anger follows."

By being a whole and happy person, or as close as you can get to it, when moving into a relationship, you will avoid this pressure and subsequent disappointment. What does it even mean to be whole? I believe it's a feeling of contentment, that you are in charge of your life, that you are happy. Perhaps we're never 100% whole, but I think the key is to ebb and flow towards it as best we can. I think it's hard to begin a relationship with someone who is in a really damaged or compromised state. I have seen it done. I just don't think it's ideal.

My stepdaughter (age 21) is a wonderful example of someone who built up her self-esteem on her own prior to dating. Having been in a relationship that was highly toxic and even dangerous, she came away from it emotionally bruised and battered. Dating was the last thing on her mind, thank goodness, because had she leaped back into the pond too quickly she would have attracted the same type of bad-news boy.

Instead, over 3 years, while going to school full time, raising a child and working part time, she slowly built back her confidence. Her self-esteem went up and, with it, the caliber of men she would consider dating. Will she ever make another bad choice? Perhaps, but her dad and I are extremely proud of the person she has become and now she knows that she's worthy of a great guy.

While this next situation probably doesn't happen all that frequently, it must be quite a blow to the mojo. Julia's story will inspire you that we can recover.

Success Story

JULIA

Life After the Bomb

My husband and I had been high school sweethearts and got married in our early 20s. We had two beautiful children, a house and a business. Things weren't always perfect, but we loved our life.

Ten years into the marriage, my husband dropped a bomb. He announced he was gay.

I was floored. It was like an earthquake had rocked my world and the floor fell out beneath me. It took me months just to digest what this actually meant for our lives as he moved out of the family home and started his new life as a single gay man.

Fortunately, there was no "other man." And I could see immediately that a huge weight had been lifted from his shoulders. His announcement had liberated him and he was literally a new man. But I couldn't help wishing that this new version of my husband was available to me! Our children took it better than I did at first, but eventually we all came around to be supportive of his life choice.

Fast-forward 10 years and our life is unusual, but it works very well for us. I have remarried and my new husband and ex get along very, very well. My ex has also married a beautiful man who we all adore.

We are one big blended family. Our children have three men in their lives and one mom and we all spend weekends and holidays together. Other people looking in say, "Really, this works for you?"

"Yep, I know it looks crazy, but we did what it took to make it work." Our children always came before our individual egos and we've figured out our new normal.

••

Julia was able to recover, regroup and ultimately get on with her life with her mojo intact. Nicely done. Every situation is going to come with its own set of issues. Julia dealt with something that many of you won't face. It could have floored her, but it didn't. There's no real rule book for how to work through a divorce, but as I've said before, the key is to recognize your feelings around it and where it's left your self-esteem. Is your mojo intact, or do you need to get to work?

Self-esteem vs. the Media

An article published by Unilever claimed that "75% of teenage girls felt 'depressed, guilty, and shameful' after spending just three minutes leafing through a fashion magazine." Is it any wonder? Even those of us who have strong self-esteem can be instantly depressed by the images of flawless skin, size 2 actresses and models. That same article also stated that the country of Fiji didn't have TV until 1995 and their young women were healthy with no eating disorders. After TV was introduced, a Harvard study found that 15% of Fijian girls were vomiting to lose weight.

Big corporations that sell into the women's market (like Unilever) have seen an opportunity here. Dove has created some really great programs for women's and girls' self-esteem and although Dove may be motivated by brand loyalty (and ultimately profits) I think they can be commended. Showing average women in their ads rather than supermodels is wonderful for the rest of us who don't look like air-brushed stick figures! If we really sat down and examined what the fashion and advertising industry has done to undermine the self-esteem of women, both young and old, I think we'd stop buying magazines all together!

Every one of us has something unique about us that we can tap into to build our mojo. So you hate your butt, but what about those amazing eyes you have? Or your gorgeous piano player hands? You are a beautiful creature and your job is to discover the things about yourself that are unique. It might not even be physical, it might be a talent that you possess, it might be kindness or maybe you're a fabulous cook! Love yourself exactly how you are today! Be kind to yourself!

When we've allowed the media and magazines to get us down, it affects our self-esteem and our mojo goes into the pooper. Let's work on that now!

*Exercise 8**
. . . .
Is Your Mojo Intact?

Answer the following questions "yes" or "no."

_____   When you look in the mirror, do you like what you see?

_____   When you walk into a room, do you do so with confidence?

_____   If asked to speak in front of a crowd of ten people, would you be able to pull it off?

_____   If a man is consistently late for dates, doesn't call when he's supposed to and takes you for granted, would you dump him?

_____   When trying on outfits at a retail store, do you look at the ones that fit you and say, "Damn, I'm rockin' this outfit?"

* Find this exercise on page 212 of *The Frog Whisperer Journal.*

If you answered "NO" to two or more questions, then your mojo may be in jeopardy. What would it take for you to build confidence? A new job? A makeover? Some exercise? Get to it! (See examples of mojo builders under Getting Your Mojo Back.)

As I said, my self-esteem had really taken a beating with The Suit. And although I waited quite awhile before dating again, I really hadn't worked on getting my mojo back. The result was The Controlling Surfer.

Frog Story
THE CONTROLLING SURFER

In my second year in Vancouver, I started to think about dating again. I'd tried a few times with no success. But finally, I did meet someone who I thought had potential.

He was from California and came with all of the traditional Californian accoutrements – blond hair, blue eyes, tanned skin. Of course he surfed, but he did have a good job. He was in Vancouver visiting a friend and we met at a bar after work one night. We laughed a lot and had a great time and a relationship began. I went to Newport Beach to visit him; he came back to Vancouver to visit me. It was going along quite nicely.

One night at dinner with some of my friends, I noticed he was always the one talking. And the stories he told were always embellished substantially so that he was constantly "one upping" everyone else. And funny enough, he was always the hero in his stories.

And when I dug a little more I started to realize that he was making all of the decisions in our relationship as well. Whether it be restaurants or movies or what we did that day – he was in charge! I had to fight to get anything my way. And to top it all off, he was a horrible listener. He was always just waiting to say what he wanted to say.

After several months of dating, I called it off. I had no desire to go through my life with this boastful egomaniac. He had a lot of the nice packaging, but the product inside sucked!

Lessons from the Frog

Have you ever heard the phrase, "You teach people how to treat you?" I think it may be a Dr. Phil-ism. This was one lesson that I wish I'd learned earlier in my dating life. But I allowed the Controlling Surfer to call the shots; I allowed him to control me. If I had said to him, "Hey, I'd really like to share in the decision-making here," he may have responded. If I had said to him, "When we're out with friends, I've noticed that you do a lot of the talking, do you realize that?" I'd at least have given him an opportunity to recognize how he was being with other people. Then, if he wasn't willing to change, I could dump him.

What I realized eventually was that when my mojo was at its lowest, I attracted men who were not even close to perfect for me.

Later in time, I started to recognize when my mojo was slipping and could take care of it more quickly, like I did with the Controlling Surfer. When I didn't feel good on the inside, my poor mojo was reflected in the types of men I would attract. They would be players, control freaks or just plain jerks.

Getting Your Mojo Back

An online self-motivation resource (www.selfmotivationresources. com/selfesteemboosters.php) provides a list of the top self-esteem boosters.

1. Compliment yourself daily.
2. Give yourself a makeover.
3. Get in shape.
4. Reward yourself.
5. Create a list of your positive aspects.

Many of these were a part of my plan. And I took #3, Get in Shape, to heart. For me it came down to physical and mental conditioning, but it might be different for you. Perhaps you have health issues, or you're in major debt (after a divorce, most people are broke!). I found that when I was in shape, I felt strong and therefore the mojo ran high. And, when I was calm and peaceful in my mind, I also felt my mojo return.

Yoga, as it turns out, is a pretty good solution for both of these factors (more on yoga a little later). But you might consider others. The key is to do what you really love so that you'll keep it up! Here's a list of potential mojo boosters. Choose the ones that suit you best based on the areas affecting your self-esteem.

Physical: Change of diet (may require expert input)
Yoga
Strength training
Tai Chi
Pilates
Self-defense classes
Martial arts
Dance
Healing hands (massage, Reiki, etc.)

Spiritual: Meditation

Church groups

Retreats

Reading

Seminars

Emotional: Journaling

Support groups

Self-esteem classes

Community involvement

Friends

Financial: Debt assistance

Coaching

Books/seminars

Note: Many of us are at an age where hormone imbalance and other physical issues have taken over our lives. If you don't feel well, start to investigate. It's difficult to get your mojo back when you aren't at 100% physically. Form a team of health care specialists (doctor, gynecologist, nutritionist, naturopath, chiropractor, etc.) to help you sort through your issues. You might be surprised at the results.

Body Image 101

We all have issues that we are facing but a good majority of us have our physical bodies intact. And that, my friends, is something to be grateful for as we move into Body Image 101.

Recently, I stumbled across a TV show from England called *How to Look Good Naked*. I had always thought it was a clever name and know that many, many people (men and women) don't like what they see in the mirror. But what you may not know is that what you see in the mirror may not be what other people see.

One show was particularly revealing. They lined up 20 women in their bras and underwear in order of waist size and asked one woman to place herself into the line where she *thought* she belonged. She placed herself two people down from the largest, when in fact, she had the smallest waist of all the people in the line. This woman had such a skewed view of her body that she even covered up the mirror in her bedroom! This is a great example because many of us might look in the mirror and see something that isn't there. Or our eyes will fixate on a problem area and miss the bigger picture.

Give yourself a break!!!

I believe that I suffered from poor body image for quite a long period in my life. As a teenager, I ballooned up quickly after The Badass left my life and continued to struggle with weight throughout my 20s and early 30s. But around my late 30s, I made a conscious effort to stop obsessing about it and it seemed to help. I stopped yo-yoing and maintained my weight. I wasn't skinny, but I just decided to be happy with being 10 or 20 pounds over what I thought was ideal.

Many of us suffer from poor body image and oftentimes what we see is not accurate.

My summer of fabulous (more on this later in the chapter) had me exercising regularly and being active. But I wasn't at any type of all-time low weight. I had learned to be comfortable in my own skin.

What's your body image? When you look in the mirror do you beat yourself up and say nasty things? Or do you say, "Yeah, pretty good for my age!" You've heard of a self-fulfilling prophecy, right? Well, if you tell yourself every day that you are fat and ugly, don't you think that you are going to step into "fat and ugly" mode after awhile? You would never speak to someone else like that, so why do you say such mean things to yourself?

Do you like how you look and feel?

If you do, then great. Embrace it. Confidence is an inside-out job. If you do not, then get to work and do something about it. Showing up fabulous means that you feel great and if shedding some pounds is what it's going to take then start your research and decide how you are going to get there.

Success Story

LOIS

Creating a New Dream When the Old One Goes South

I was 19 when I married my high school sweetheart. Determined that our two children would not become casualties of a broken home, I persevered with this love-hate marriage for 13 years. It takes guts to call it quits, and start over. But, I knew what I needed to do. I divorced him and promised myself that "if" I ever remarried, it would be for money, not love.

But I met Larry, and fell in love anyway. We eloped a short while later. But our wedded bliss quickly collided with our new reality. A huge utility truck violently crashed into my car and shattered our life's plans. A brain injury left me a shell of the woman who had married Larry just 9 months earlier. But we hung on and, slowly, my condition improved.

We both love to use wit and humor to make each other laugh, to reset stressful emotions and to cheer each other up. The first years of my rehabilitation, I didn't feel like laughing. I felt angry because life cheated me out of my future plans, sad for my loss and justified in feeling sorry for myself. Larry made me laugh when I thought I couldn't. He made me feel loved.

Acknowledging that we were newlyweds in a second marriage with blended family challenges ahead of us, part of my on-going therapy was to spend intimate time with my husband twice a week. Our intention was simply to enjoy each other and our time together.

We still practice this habit 19 years later. Every week, Larry and I take time out from the unpredictable swift pace of life to cuddle, and just hang out together. Our top priority is to spend meaningful time with each other, and our children ... to fully appreciate our uniqueness and have fun together.

••

I included Lois' story because it gives us some perspective. In my line of work as a coach for professional speakers, I have coached people with many disabilities. Imagine having no arms or no legs or being blind. Imagine spending your life in a wheelchair with a disease that attacks your body every day, or having a brain injury. The next time you look into the mirror and complain about your butt being big or your muffin top, give your head a shake and remember Lois!

Yoga – Good for Mind and Body

I found a great mojo booster that worked for me. Yoga provided fitness for my body and calm for my mind. It allowed me to quiet all the chatter and I have a busy, busy mind! I'm constantly thinking, worrying, planning. And yoga allowed me just to be in a state of peace.

While you are going through your "get happy" process, removing some of the toxic things in your life, you may consider taking up a practice that will help keep you grounded and feeling peaceful (and even taller!).

People all over the world are taking up yoga. Here in my hometown, even young boys in school are doing it – possibly just to "get chicks," who really knows? Yoga can make you feel more in touch with your body, stronger and, most importantly (in my mind), help quiet your inner voice. You know that constant chattering that goes on in your head when you are trying to concentrate in a big meeting or when trying to get to sleep at night? For some of us, that inner voice never shuts up!

When I was living in Dallas, a girlfriend told me, "I just came from the best workout I've ever had! It's called Bikram Yoga. They heat up the yoga studio to over 100 degrees." By putting this much heat in the room, it allows your muscles to be their most flexible.

"That sounds awful," I said.

"You'd think it would be and at first I couldn't concentrate because of the heat, but once I got past that it was incredible!" She was glowing as she said this so I thought why not give it a shot.

My first class was possibly the most uncomfortable 90 minutes of my life. While sweating profusely, 40 people twisted themselves into slippery pretzel-type poses. But I remembered the instructor saying something about not letting anything steal your peace. I was determined to get through an entire class without bitching (in my head) about the heat and conditions. So I went back.

After about three classes, I was hooked. Each time, the heat made me feel like I had been through a detox or cleanse. And over the course of about 2 years, I watched people in that studio transform. A mother of six dropped 20 pounds. A lawyer, who came to class nearly every day, grew his hair back! He must have lost it due to stress. And for me, I felt more fit, which was nice, but the main benefit was that my mind calmed down. At the end of each class, while lying in the Savasana (resting position), I had a clear mind. I didn't think about getting back to work, I didn't think about what I was going to eat after I left and I didn't think about the crazy heat in that room. My mind was calm.

If you're at all menopausal, you might want to try a non-heated yoga, but if you think you can take it, hot yoga can be a great workout with positive mental effects.

Lifting Your Spirit

By now you've heard of *Eat, Pray, Love* (bestseller turned movie). After a nasty divorce, Elizabeth Gilbert went on a 1-year journey to find herself. She started in Italy, with 4 months of eating great food and speaking Italian. Then she went to India and learned yoga and meditation to help her calm her mind and get in touch with her spirit. Then she went to Indonesia. This was where she fell in love. It was only after everything was right in her body and soul that her perfect mate showed up. Gilbert's book is so inspiring to anyone who is getting back on their feet.

The meditation part of Liz's story inspired me to start my own practice again. I have never been great at things that required discipline, but I know that this one is worth the effort for the sheer effects of the quieting of the mind.

Meditation could be called "prayer" if that works for you. Or it could be called "sitting still," as in, "Honey, call me back in 20 minutes. I'm sitting still right now." It doesn't matter. The purpose is to calm and clear your mind. Sometimes you might concentrate on a certain mantra while you are meditating.

Swami Sivananda says, "Meditation is painful in the beginning but it bestows immortal bliss and supreme joy in the end."

*Exercise 9**
. . . .
Quieting the Mind

I'll give you my very non-technical approach to meditation. There are many different practices that you can learn and apply; this is just a basic one to get you started. The key word is "practice" because if you do it only once a month, chances are you won't see great results.

* Find this exercise on page 231 of *The Frog Whisperer Journal.*

Try it for 5 minutes the first time out and slowly increase to 20 minutes. Daily is the best practice, but let's take it in small steps. You may want to set an alarm so you don't have to look at the clock.

Step 1. Find a quiet place where you won't be disturbed.

Step 2. Get into a relaxed position. A comfy chair is fine. Sit in a position that feels comfortable to you, palms up. Keep in mind you don't really want to fall asleep.

Step 3. Close your eyes and concentrate on your breathing – deeply in and all the way out.

Step 4. As you breathe, focus on a word, like "love" or "peace." Imagine love washing over you and how that might feel.

Pretty easy, right?

The goal is to give your mind a break from all of the normal, everyday thoughts and worries. If thoughts enter your head while you are meditating, just let them go and come back to your focus word. That word will allow you to focus on something positive. If you are able to take up a practice on a regular basis, you will notice that you have more calm in your life, that you have more clarity. Some people claim that they have things come to them more quickly when they meditate – this is manifestation at its finest. I won't make any claims for you – I just hope you can carve out a few minutes each day to calm your mind and feel peaceful.

Meditation isn't for everybody. For me, it's hard to keep up the practice on a regular basis, but I think when we want to change something in our life, we try everything! To learn how to meditate properly you might find a book, an audio or take a class. *The Frog Whisperer Positive Practice* Audio could also be a great place to start.

Working with an Olympic Athlete for 4 years was very helpful in terms of learning about the power of the mind. In his book *The Ant and the Elephant,* Vince Poscente (www.vinceposcente.com) says that your conscious mind is the ant, and the elephant is your subconscious mind. And if you learn to control the more powerful portion of your mind (the elephant) then you tap into your potential more fully. You'll read more about this later in this chapter at Love Mantras. Dating all the way back to authors like Napoleon Hill (*Think and Grow Rich*), people have been teaching us that our thoughts dictate our outcomes.

Do you believe that?

Now, I don't want to get into all of the metaphysics surrounding this topic (I'll let *The Secret* do that for you), but suffice it to say that scientists have actually proven that thoughts contain power. In the book *The Hidden Messages in Water* by Masaru Emoto, a group of people gathered around a body of water and prayed, sending the water positive thoughts. Another group of people surrounded the same body of water, but prayed nasty, negative thoughts. The frozen crystals were examined under a microscope after each instance and the outcome was staggering. The crystals exposed to loving words showed brilliant, complex and colorful patterns while the water exposed to negative thoughts formed incomplete, asymmetrical patterns with dull colors.

So imagine that if you go through life sending out negative vibes, what is that doing for you? What is that doing for your love life? If you make the statement, even subconsciously, "I'll never find anyone good" or "There are no good men out there," you are creating something negative for yourself. Or worse, you're attracting crappy people.

Lightening Your Emotional Baggage – Radical Forgiveness

Another big step in getting your mojo back is easing your load or letting go of all the emotional stuff that's holding you back. What do you need to let go of to move forward in your life?

Another big step in getting your mojo back is lightening your emotional baggage.

Years ago I stumbled across a program called Radical Forgiveness (www.radicalforgiveness.com). At the time, I didn't realize how much I was holding inside and that it was eating me up. Taking a weekend course, I learned a technique that was really helpful in diffusing situations that held a lot of negative energy. It was fascinating how quickly it worked. I got rid of a lot of baggage and still remember to use the technique when I'm struggling with a situation. (You'd be surprised at how many fires can be put out with forgiveness.)

One of the key premises of radical forgiveness is that it's not really about the story around the situation; it's about the energy that you have given to that story. When you move past the energy and look for the lesson in the situation, it frees you up. Here's an example.

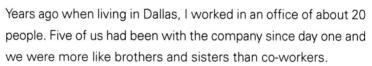

Success Story

JANE

Forgive and Profit

Years ago when living in Dallas, I worked in an office of about 20 people. Five of us had been with the company since day one and we were more like brothers and sisters than co-workers.

Well, one of my brothers was really getting on my nerves and I built up a lot of anger and resentment towards him. (The usual workplace bickering type stuff.) With the way our commissions were set up, if he booked my speakers, I would make money; if he didn't, I didn't make money. So it was really in my best interests to make peace with my brother.

After a few months of growing resentment, I decided to put my 13 Radical Forgiveness steps to work on the situation. When I really looked at what had occurred – the actual deeds that went down, not the emotions I made up about those events – there was very little left. By scraping away the emotions (what I had made up about the story) I was able to see the reality and I let my anger go. The big lesson for me was that I could exhibit some of the same behaviors that had so annoyed me coming from him. Funny enough, the next morning he showed up at my office door with a multi-speaker deal in hand. Cha-ching! Thank you radical forgiveness.

Letting go takes practice, and for some people it might seem impossible. But try to look at how much negative energy you have added to a situation, and the story that you've built around that energy. Let's work through an example.

Your husband cheated on you in a one-night stand with a girl he met in a bar. Over the months following this event you build up a case of years of betrayal, your whole marriage is a lie, he's a rotten father, everything out of his mouth is tainted, he's a scumbag, low-life who has stolen your youth and broken your heart.

As hard as it may be, try to scrape away all of the emotions you've added to the situation and look at what's really true. Don't turn one night of betrayal into an entire lifetime of lies, unless that's actually true. (It's hard to do, right?) Could he have made a mistake and is contrite about it now? Or were there issues in the marriage that had him seeking attention elsewhere? It may be that he's really just a scumbag, and if he is, then be glad you don't have to spend the rest of your life with him! He did you a favor. But he may simply be a man who made a mistake. Try to see what's true.

I know I'm picking a sensitive subject here, but Radical Forgiveness is just that – radical. It takes a lot of work to dull the emotions of betrayal, but the results can be quite amazing. If you feel the need to work on forgiveness, I'd highly recommend checking into the work of Colin Tipping (www.radicalforgiveness.com).

Getting Your Emotions Out – Write It Down

Writing has always been a source of emotional release for me. If something keeps me awake at night, I get up and write about it. A good example of this practice was our house purchase about 6 months before John and I got married.

We had to sell two homes and buy one home all within a very short time frame. Certainly there were things that could go wrong in a situation like that. But when I found myself stuck in worry mode about it, I wrote it all out exactly as I wanted it to happen. Sure enough, it all went smoothly!

Writing is a really effective emotional release. You can be honest with your words, and you probably won't edit yourself like you might in therapy. If you're angry, you can write and write until it's all outside of your body (a very healthy thing to do, by the way).

I journal about everything. At the beginning of the year, I'll write down all my goals and a plan to achieve them. My journals are my babies, I have some from 10 years ago that I still go back and review. It's wonderful to see how much has come true.

I've heard Oprah talk about journaling. I believe she keeps a gratitude journal. Every day you write down what you are grateful for. I quite like this one because even if you had a bad day, you can always find something to write down – food on the table, shelter overhead, family, my dog.

If you don't have a *Frog Whisperer Journal*, get a blank book with a cover that appeals to you – flowers, puppies, a mountain scene. See what works for you – writing first thing in the morning about your hopes for the day ahead or in the evening to express your thanks for a great day. Perhaps writing once a week would suffice. Whatever helps. Journaling isn't for everyone, but you won't know until you give it a try.

Show Me the Money

When moving into a relationship, you need to be able to stand on your own financially, rather than being saved. I'm not saying you need to be wealthy, but just make sure you're not turning towards someone out of need.

Our friends Dan and Stacy just split up. Stacy was very young and influenced by money when she and Dan first got together. He took charge of things and earned a better-than-average living. And now 10 years and 2 children later she wants a divorce. It's no longer about the money and security. She wants out so that she can find herself. The old saying "money can't buy happiness" keeps coming back because it's always going to be true.

There are a million great advisers on money, Suze Orman, Jean Chatzky. What I like about Suze's approach is that it comes from a spiritual place of being truthful about your finances, not trying to put on a show (that is false) for the world. If you're in Canada, make sure you get a book that applies to Canadians. I hear that Gail Vaz-Oxlade is good.

By taking steps to control your own financial destiny, you are moving into the best place possible. When someone is in control of your money, they are in control of your life. Even if you enter a relationship, make sure that you stay in control. For instance, John and I have a joint account for paying the mortgage and some bills, but we both keep our own bank accounts and credit cards (this is what Suze Orman recommends).

Sometimes we might feel good leaning on someone. But when it comes to money, we should feel great about being in charge of our decisions and our destiny. And when you feel in charge of your money, you feel great about yourself and therefore are putting out some strong, positive vibes!

Almost Set

So we're READY. We know who we are and what we want. And we've got our psyche SET; we're feeling happy in our own skin. Before we move on to setting our stage, I want to share a frog story from way back. This one's right out of a Taylor Swift heartbreak song.

Frog Story
THE BADASS

I first laid eyes on The Badass when I was 13 years old. I was at gymnastics practice, up on the balance beam, and he and my brother sauntered into the gym at 7 p.m. to pick me up. He caught my eye in mid-cartwheel and I nearly fell off. Yowza! He was 20 at the time, tall, gorgeous brown curly hair, smoldering hazel eyes and broad shoulders. He had a George Clooney essence about him and the voice to match. That night was the beginning of a crush that would later turn into a teenage obsession and then a lesson – a big lesson.

I saw him on and off through the years and at around age 16, The Badass and I were at a party together. I was no saint and partying had become second nature. I had my share of Daddy issues at that time, and I was looking for love in all the wrong places.

I don't recall exactly how we got together, but I will say that looking back on it, a 23-year-old has no business hooking up with a 16-year-old. It was simply wrong. But we dated secretly for about 6 months. He took flak from his siblings who said he was "robbing the cradle" and I ended up losing all of my friends over the relationship.

Every night I would wait at home for him to call around 7 p.m., meanwhile, everyone else would make plans and go out for the night. Sometimes he called, more often he didn't. I had to be there to answer the phone, because if my parents found out I was dating this guy, I'd be in trouble.

What I learned later on was that while I was waiting by the phone and falling hard for The Badass, he was out in the bars partying and sleeping with a different girl every night. At the end of 6 months, he didn't call and say we shouldn't see each other anymore, he just stopped calling. I felt used and tossed aside and cried for days and started drowning my sorrows in Häagen-Dazs.

After a couple of weeks of this, and even some crazy thoughts of suicide, I made a decision that would go on to affect me for years. I made a pact with myself that I would never cry over another man again. Looking back I think that was quite pivotal and it took years to shake the aftermath of The Badass.

Incidentally, The Badass turned out to be a worse character than I even imagined. He turned to crime and drugs and I heard that he ended up dying at a young age under mysterious circumstances in a New York hotel room.

Lessons from the Frog

This frog metamorphized into a multi-lesson journey! And it took awhile to get through them all.

The first major lesson was around forgiveness. I could have let The Badass dictate my life and my relationships even to this day, but forgiveness had to happen. Heck, we were both very young and very selfish.

Often things that we dislike about someone are traits that we possess ourselves. I recognize now that many of the negatives that he revealed at that time were characteristics that I have possessed on and off throughout my life. I've certainly been selfish, thoughtless and hurtful towards people – much less now than before.

The next lesson was that when everyone around you thinks your guy is bad news, then you need to take a long, hard look at that situation. All of his friends and my friends thought we were crazy and my parents would definitely not have approved. When I'm in stubborn mode, like I was at that time (what 16-year-old isn't?), I wanted what I wanted and nothing was going to deter me. I didn't want to listen. I couldn't hear anyone.

> When everyone around you is saying something negative, open your mind to what might be true; allow yourself to see what's real, not just what you want to see.

So, if you're a young person, or a stubborn person, please hear this … When everyone around you is saying something negative, open your mind to what might be true; allow yourself to see what's real, not just what you want to see.

Chances are you are turning a blind eye to something and it may save you some pain to be more aware of what's true.

Another positive was that my "Player Radar" was turned on and has stayed on my entire dating life. The Badass was a huge player and I was able to recognize players a lot easier later in my life as a result. The key was gaining back enough self-esteem to resist the players and that would be a work in progress until well into my 30s.

As I've said, we've all got wounds – some big, some small but mighty. Recognizing which wounds are pivotal in our lives is the first step to healing them.

Jane's Summer of Fabulous

Early one spring I decided, "This is it. This is my year to find true love." I set out to make changes in my life, including getting happy. I knew I had to do that before taking that big giant *leap* into love. So my Summer of Fabulous plan started to take shape. I asked myself, "What would really make me happy?"

First, I needed to look into that little cottage I had been craving. Spending time with The Fishmonger drew me even closer to the lake, and now I had to act. I also knew that being physically active would keep those endorphins flowing and would continue to boost my mojo. Dating The Fishmonger had really helped me boost my self-esteem, so I had a good start. I also needed to surround myself with people and things that I loved. So off I went … into my Summer of Fabulous.

By making the cottage purchase, I was taking control of my destiny. I could have waited to try to buy a place with a partner, but there were no guarantees that I was going to get into a relationship anytime soon. I needed to do this to carry out my plan. So I went shopping and found a little shack that needed a lot of TLC. It was right in my price range and, although it wasn't very glamorous, it put me right where I wanted to be, at the lake!

For the first few months of that summer, my cottage neighbors said it was like watching a home makeover show. I brought in all of the things I loved – a water fountain, two comfy chairs on the front porch, candles and a fireplace. I made that rundown little shack my own and felt very proud of it.

That was *Step 1* in the Summer of Fabulous – setting up the space I loved. (More on setting up your space later.)

Step 2 was getting off of my butt.

I bought a bike. Not an expensive bike, in fact Walmart had a special deal going. But I did invest in a comfortable seat. Every morning at the cottage, I woke up and either went for a walk or a bike ride before beginning my workday. As a coach and consultant, working at the cottage was easy for me; all I need for my business to run is a phone and a computer line and I put in both especially for my Summer of Fabulous.

Step 3 was surrounding myself with people I wanted to spend time with.

In the past, I had developed relationships with other girls based on the fact that they were single too. No more. I wanted friendships that were rich. I wanted to be around positive people who felt that finding love was indeed possible. I limited my time with people who were toxic or negative about life.

Step 4 was to be happy.

There might have been a tinge of loneliness in the things that I did that summer, but I did things that made me happy. I walked along the beach a lot, I watched the sunsets, I went for drinks with friends and basically had an extremely relaxed summer. It was a summer of solitude and reflection and at the end of that time, I came away feeling happy about my life.

These four steps were actually the final phases of putting my plan into action. I had been working toward this point for some time. I'd started at the beginning of the year with something that I do every New Year's Day.

Documenting the Dream

One practice that I started years ago was building a dream board for every new year. Over the holidays, I sit down with a bunch of my favorite magazines and my laptop and start cutting out pictures of all of the things that I like, resonate with or want in my life. Sometimes I'd use clip art, or find an image that spoke to me. Sometimes it's just a pretty picture that makes me feel happy when I look at it, sometimes it's something that I want to acquire, like a new watch or shoes. Often, it's something I want to accomplish, like writing a book. I also add words to the board to show the theme of my year. Last year was love, for instance, whereas this year is health and wealth. So, where last year there were photos of happy couples, this year there are photos of healthy food, yoga and bars of gold.

I remember when watching *The Secret* one of the experts talked about a time in his life where he had put his dream board away in a box for many years and had moved several times. And when he dug it out again, he realized that a photo of a house he had cut out from a magazine was the exact home he had purchased.

A colleague of mine, Murray Smith, who co-wrote *The Answer: Grow Any Business, Achieve Financial Freedom, and Live an Extraordinary Life*, works his dream board every day. Murray says that putting up a dream board isn't enough; you have to look at it every day and take actions that will move you closer to creating your dream.

I still do a dream board every year, but now I place it in a beautiful frame with a mat and have invited my stepdaughters to do their boards at the same time. It's great to see what they set out as goals for themselves each year.

Love Mantras

My old boss, Olympic Speed Skier Vince Poscente, had a process for locking in a mantra that was quite effective for him getting to the Olympics. He called it the "yellow dot" theory.

Vince was considered old (age 35) when he made the decision to go out for the Canadian Olympic team in the sport of speed skiing. Now I know 35 isn't old, but he was competing against guys who were 20!

He had to be one of the top ten skiers in the world in order to qualify. So aside from physical and mental training, he created a mantra for himself – "I am the fastest speed skier in Canada, top ten in the world." Vince had never competed before, so the idea seemed unthinkable, but his brain didn't know that.

He purchased a package of yellow dots from Staples (the kind that are about the size of a pencil eraser) and set about putting them everywhere. When he opened his wallet, he'd see the dot and repeat his mantra to himself, "I'm the fastest speed skier in Canada, top ten in the world." He'd go to the refrigerator and see the dot – "I'm the fastest speed skier in Canada, top ten in the world." He'd get in his car, look in the rearview mirror, see the dot and – "I'm the fastest speed skier in Canada, top ten in the world."

Eventually, Vince became the fastest speed skier in Canada and top ten in the world. The mantra worked!

I've used mantras in my own life and they've been very helpful. Staying open to love was the one that I used as a part of my Summer of Fabulous. It went something like this: "I am a happy, attractive woman who is open to love." I put the yellow dots all over my condo, in my car and at my cottage. People who came to visit would say, "What's up with all the dots?" I'd just reply, "Oh, that's just how I remind myself of something." And leave it at that.

When creating a mantra it's important how you structure it. It's best to put it into positive terms. Rather than "I am no longer a negative person" a mantra should be more like "I am a joyful person who thinks positive thoughts." Try to use words that feel good to you.

Mantras are meant to be a stretch. For instance, I've used mantras around wealth, long before I had money. It might have been something like "I am a happy, healthy and wealthy woman." I might not have had two nickels to rub together at the time, but guess what? My brain didn't know that! And eventually, it came true. I want you to be aware that the mantra (like many of these ideas) is not the "quick fix" to your relationship issues; they are all ideas that can point you in the right direction. You still need to do the work! Sorry!

Who's in Your Corner?

Over the years, I've been really conscious of being around people who support my dreams. Who's in your corner helping you to bring your dreams to life?

Are you surrounded by naysayers or people who say, "That sounds like a terrific plan." If you find yourself being showered in cold water whenever you speak with your friend, your sister, your mother or a co-worker, then get smart about it. Be careful who you share your dreams with because negative people will rain on your parade every time.

If you don't have people in your world who are supportive, then seek them out. Creating a support group, like a Frog Whisperer Club (see Girl Power and Exercise 5, The Frog Whisperer Book Club in Step 1), is a great first step. Recognize who your dream stealers are and limit your time with them. When it's family, you may have to see them, but you don't have to share everything that's going on in your life with them.

Pop my balloon once, shame on you. Pop my balloon many times, shame on me.

Let's get smart about who we trust with our dreams.

Showing Up!

One of my life coaches, Chris, is something of a visionary – some would even call him psychic. It drives me crazy because I'll show up to a meeting thinking I can fool him into believing I feel better about myself than I really do and he calls me to the mat. Let's just say he reads my body language and tells me exactly how I am really feeling. No BS there.

Back when I first met Chris at a business event, he told me that he'd never seen someone trying so hard to look invisible. And that was exactly what I was doing, trying to blend into the scenery. I had convinced myself that I was a behind-the-scenes person and didn't need the spotlight. I wasn't aware that I was trying to hide but becoming aware was a big step. After a few months of working with him, I started to realize that I wasn't living up to my potential in several areas and I wanted to make some changes.

Later that year at a convention in Phoenix, something changed. I had been attending these conferences for nearly 15 years. But this year, I arrived in a different state of mind, mojo intact. I decided to wear a killer red dress to the final night gala. It was a big deal – black tie – most people went all out with tuxes and gowns. Usually, I'd wear a black cocktail dress or something pretty conservative, but this night was special. I felt good and I was ready to share it!

The results were quite amazing. It was as if some of the people who I'd seen at this same event for all those years were just seeing me for the first time. It felt as though, rather than blending in, I was actually "showing up!" I felt very strong and confident wearing that killer dress. I was walking down the hallway at the hotel going to the dance and people kept stopping me to say how amazing I looked. I just smiled, knowing my secret, and said, "Thank you." Thanks to coach Chris, I now notice how I am "being in the world." That night, I was a superstar.

Showing up might come in different forms for everyone. For some of you, just getting out of your home is a big step. "Showing up" at a social event when you would much rather be in front of your TV watching *The Bachelorette* and eating Cheetos can be daunting. Showing up might be in the form of stepping out of your comfort zone to take charge on a project at work. Or maybe it's giving a speech. Showing up is a way of being that says "I'm present and I'm ready to live my life more fully." For me, showing up in the red dress said, "Hey everybody, I'm here and I'm fabulous!" But everyone will have their own version to work on and it may change as you grow and evolve.

To me the biggest compliment someone could give is saying, "You look different, did you change something?" When they can't really pinpoint it, perhaps it's because you showed up differently.

But for some people, like Karen, showing up, even when you are distracted, could also work.

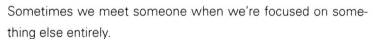

KAREN

When You Least Expect It

Sometimes we meet someone when we're focused on something else entirely.

My friend Karen met her husband online about 9 years ago. She had been married twice before and her husband had also been married with kids. All of their children were grown up and gone from their homes, so they were empty nesters.

Prior to meeting him, Karen had started a new job that was very demanding and stressful. There didn't seem to be any time for a personal life. She worked long days, and fell into bed after late dinners alone at home.

On the odd occasion, Karen would have a peek at dating sites. Just knowing people were out there made her feel better. And after one particularly exhausting week at work, she decided to post a profile for fun.

Because of her hectic schedule, she didn't spend any time on men who didn't meet her criteria: good sense of humor, fit, good core values, like sports and not bad looking. She had several coffee dates that didn't pan out, so she just continued to focus on her 50-hour work-week. One day Greg wrote to her and Karen was impressed by how much he sounded like her! They met for drinks at a local pub and they both knew right away that this was something different. It really was WOW.

They recently sat in the same booth where they first met and celebrated their 9th anniversary from their first meeting. They've now been married for 4 years. She says, "This is the BEST time of my life."

While she was focused in another direction, love found her and Karen has never been happier!

Get Set in Your Space for Success

Have you ever heard of feng shui, pronounced "fung shway?" For several years I have incorporated it into the homes that I've purchased. Basically, it's about energy flowing through your home and using different things like water and colors to improve different areas of your life. Karen Rauch Carter states that feng shui is an ancient Chinese art form that creates harmony and balance in your environment so that it fully supports you in life.

She helps people remove barriers to energy, open up flow and get their spaces into a more positive (and often visually appealing) mode.

A while back, I flipped on the *Nate Berkus Show* and they were talking about what might turn off a potential partner in your home. This one girl had kitty litter boxes in her bedroom *and* spare room. Yikes, that might send someone packing pretty quick! It's okay to have cats, but you need to think about setting up your bedroom with a partner in mind. And there ain't nothing romantic (or feng shui) about a stinky litter box!

My favorite book (by Karen) on the topic is called *Move Your Stuff, Change Your Life* (www.karenrauchcarter.com). Love it! Karen has a fun style and doesn't take herself too seriously. I reread the book at the beginning of my Summer of Fabulous and set about changing up the atmosphere in my condo and at my new cottage.

Once again, it's about creating the right energy. It's quite easy to move a few things around to become more partner-centered rather than single-centered. For instance, in my bedroom, I had the bed right up against the wall so that only one person could get in and out of it comfortably. Being partner focused, I moved the bed to the middle of the wall and added a bedside table to the other side. I also got rid of a lot of the clutter underneath my bed. (Clutter is never good and serves no purpose.) In the relationship corner, I added some colors (reds and pinks) and put candles into pairs.

I also made some changes at my cottage. I had incorporated a fountain into the front porch. I moved that into the relationship corner. Funny story about that, though … in late summer I was telling my friends Tina and Tim who were visiting one weekend about what was happening in my love life. Basically men were coming and going but no one was "the one." When I told them about the fountain, I also complained that the fountain had a leak that I needed to fix. Well, duh!!! My relationship corner was a direct reflection of what was going on in my life. Once I plugged the leaky hole in the fountain, it was only a few weeks before John came into my life. That might sound like a coincidence to you – maybe it was, *but maybe not.*

Before the cottage deal had even closed, I had purchased two large rattan chairs that I envisioned on the front porch of the cottage. They had really great comfy cushions and were the epitome of relaxation. I knew I would sit in those chairs on that front porch with my partner, long before he even came along! I also bought two coffee mugs with hearts on them. And sure enough, fast-forward about 6 months after making these purchases, John comes along and we spend every Saturday and Sunday morning sipping coffee in those cozy chairs on the front porch of our little getaway.

Find out something about feng shui and you can easily make some changes to your space that will set you up for long-term relationship success.

You might think some of this stuff sounds hokey, but what if you tried it and it worked? Would you still care that it seems hokey?

Beach Weekend – Letting Go

My girlfriend Kris flew in from Minneapolis for Labor Day weekend. We planned a chicks' weekend and rented a bigger cottage right beside the beach, complete with a hot tub! Kris had just gone through a very painful divorce so she was coming to lick her wounds and recapture her mojo. We spent the days lying on the beach and going for long walks and in the evenings we cooked amazing dinners and drank wine. Afterwards, we hit the bar. And oh my gosh, we hit it hard!

There was a college basketball team that seemed to take to us and we were surrounded by "the tall boys" on the dance floor the entire weekend. We drank, we laughed and we had fun without once thinking, "Hey, does this guy like me? Maybe I could have a relationship with him."

That would have been seriously delusional since we were 20 years older than those college kids! Nope, we weren't there for that – we were there strictly to have fun! Although we had no desire to be "cougars," I'm pretty sure we could have dragged any number of those tall boys back to the hot tub, but we didn't. We went back and soaked our dance weary bones and laughed about the night. We had so much fun.

When I look back at that weekend, I realize we were both letting go of a lot of our old patterns. We let go of the need to be "liked" by the tall boys. We let go of the need to keep the party going. But most importantly, we let go of some old attitudes that weren't serving us.

At the end of the weekend, Kris and I went down to the beach with pen and paper in hand and a BBQ lighter. We were going to perform our Letting Go Ritual. Each of us wrote down the things that we were going to let go of in our lives. I don't know what Kris wrote, but my list had a few things like "I'm letting go of being so comfortable being alone … I'm letting go of playing small and safe in my life… I'm letting go of being emotionally unavailable … etc."

I had my mojo intact and I was now ready to let go of being single. It was the perfect ending to a nearly perfect Summer of Fabulous.

I was READY and SET to LEAP.

Two weeks later, I met John.

Timing Really IS Everything

My Summer of Fabulous had worked to move me into a contented, happy space. I truly believe that had everything to do with meeting Mr. Right. In fact, John and I had chatted online several months earlier and then he just flaked. We didn't have a date set or anything, but he didn't get back to me to schedule one.

As it turns out, I wasn't ready when we connected the first time in the spring. I still had work to do. And John was still pretty tangled up in his old relationship as well. So when he came back around in the fall, I had to override my normal "closed off" desire to kick his butt to the curb for flaking on me the first time. Remember my new mantra about "staying open to love?" This was what kicked in to give him a second chance.

And well, the rest is history. Timing really saved us. We both agree that had we met at the beginning of the summer, chances are we wouldn't be together today.

Beach Follow-Up

Remember Kris and I burning our list of things we were letting go of on the beach? Well, I didn't ask her at the time what was on her list. She was going through a really rough divorce and I knew she would tell me when she was ready. We finally talked about it 18 months later, after she'd had an especially crazy period (including losing the home she was living in and planning to buy) and here's what she said …

Success Story

KRIS

Imagining Big!

After the divorce (and that day on the beach) I let go of looking at life the way I always had. I really wanted to see life the way I was meant to – using all my potential to do the things that I'm really good at and that will serve others.

I knew I needed to shed some people, and what I call "barnacles" before I would feel free enough to see what life had in store for the "new me." The beach was a big moment for me because it was a stake in the ground. I was on my way.

Since then I just smile when things happen that don't seem like they are good things, like losing the condo and having to pack and move in 4 days. My stuff is in storage and I've never felt more *in* my life! Thanks to great friends, I have a chance to live in a beautiful place practically free for a year while I wait to find the place that really feels like home to me.

I've also let go of the need to have a man in my life. I know that I have a lot to give. But right now I'm busy learning what it means to really put myself first. I'm proud of how I raised my kids, and took care of my sick mom for so many years. But doing that while creating a new career (and being married to someone I barely saw) took its toll. I took care of myself but I really didn't know what it was to concentrate on what was best for me.

It's a wild ride I'm on and I've only just begun.

I think the end of this story, if there ever is one, will be more exciting than I can currently imagine. Imagining *big* is what I'm working on now.

Ideas to Ponder

You may want to take action on these one at a time.

- What are your true feelings and perceptions about love? Will they get you where you want to go?

- Has your mojo taken a hit? If so, what steps might you take to get it back?

- What's your body image? Do you need to take action in order to feel better about yourself?

- Try journaling for 2 weeks. Each day write down what you are grateful for and notice how this changes your attitude.

- Make a note of the people in your life who are dream stealers. Take steps to surround yourself with positive, supportive people.

- Who do you need to forgive in your life? Recognize and take steps toward it (i.e., Radical Forgiveness).

- What do you need to let go of? Write down your list and perhaps hold your own beach ceremony. If you're burning your list, be sure to do it safely.

- What needs to go on your dream board? Get your computer and those magazines out and get to work!

- What needs to change in your surroundings to incorporate another person into your life? Pick up your feng shui book and start moving things around (don't worry, it won't take long).

- What's your mantra for successfully finding love? Start to develop language that feels good for you.

- How will you show up to your life?

Are You Set?

Step 1 (READY) was about getting ready to be open to love and creating a vision for our future. We had to be in a place where we could identify the patterns and do some self-examination. Not an easy step.

But Step 2 (SET) has been even tougher. We had to get our psyche set – work on the things that were holding us back – and then set up our life and our environment to be happy and fabulous.

Step 3 (LEAP) may be the toughest of all. Now we have to get off the lily pad and take the leap into the dating world. But don't worry, I have some tips that will help you feel more confident navigating the dating scene.

STEP 3 – LEAP

Getting Out There

"You're not going to attract the person who is right for
you until you become a whole person yourself."
Jim Carrey

In this section, we're going to take our fabulous selves out to the dating world. I'll provide you with some tools that will help you move through that world with more ease. Having had many, many coffee dates, I feel a strong expertise in this area!

While taking the leap might feel scary at first, I think once you have your knowledge in hand, you're going to view this as fun!

Venturing Off the Lily Pad

Dating is scary. There is no question that putting yourself out there is an uncomfortable prospect. Especially if you've ever had a bad blind date – or perhaps worse – had an invitation turned down. See how Lisa persevered and lived to LEAP again.

Success Story

LISA

Ask and They Will Answer

This is an old story, but relevent. My story began years ago in college.

Have you ever made eye contact with someone across a room and just felt the chemistry? Well, that happened to me and I didn't tell anyone about it. For months I kept locking eyes with a young man across the cafeteria and study hall. It seemed that whenever I looked up, he was looking at me, and vice versa. After months of following him with my eyes and hoping he would be in the rooms when I was, I finally confessed my obsession to my friend. She observed us and gave a resounding "Yes!" He was looking at me as much as I was looking at him.

Not having a lot of confidence with boys back then, I didn't do anything about it. As the last few weeks of the school year came around, my friend urged me to get over it and make the first move. I was terrified, because he was always surrounded by his group of friends. Well, on the last day of school, as he got up with his friends to leave the cafeteria, I made my move.

I caught him in the hallway, called his name, and in front of eight other guys, I asked him out. Here was his reply: "I'd love to ... *but* ... I'm getting married in three weeks."

You can imagine the size of the ball of lead that hit my stomach. I was so embarrassed in front of his friends. I don't even remember how fast I scooted out of there or where I went; I just hightailed it. I don't know how guys do this all the time! It was my friend who turned me around with this very true observation.

She said, "What are you embarrassed about? Do you know how flattered he must be that a girl stopped him in front of his friends and asked him out? He's probably a hero right now. Especially because he's getting married and girls are still chasing him."

That just made so much sense. Instead of feeling embarrassed and thinking I wasn't good enough, I thought, "Yeah! I just made his day!" Breaking through that fear to ask a guy out and realizing it didn't kill me was really powerful.

A year later, I met a young man at a party thrown by my dear friend Dauphne. I had heard about him for months because he was the best friend of Dauphne's boyfriend. Unfortunately, whenever I heard about him and how perfect we would be together and how we had the same bizarre sense of humor, Dauphne would say, "But he's too shy to talk to girls." And that would be the end of that.

Somehow, we ended up at a party together and indeed, he kept me in stitches all night. Knowing he was shy, I managed to make a good move at the right time so that instead of his friend driving him home, I did. After all, it was along the way for me. We hit it off but when I dropped him off, he just didn't have the nerve to ask me out.

Two days later, I said to myself, "Lisa, you asked before and you did it in front of a group, and it didn't kill you. It won't kill you to try again." I picked up the phone and called him. What was his answer? No.

He had a bad cold and couldn't go out. I was crushed. I thought it would work this time. Somehow, I kept the spark of hope alive and 3 days later, he called back and we went out. Six months later, I asked him to marry me and we got married 2 months after that. We have had 25 wonderful years, four wonderful children and lots of laughter.

What were my lessons? If you don't ask, people don't have the opportunity to say yes!!

I have never been afraid to ask for what I want since.

When it comes to dating and rejection, there is a book that I believe helps put things into perspective. It's called *He's Just Not That Into You*. When I read this book, it was like a breath of fresh air. And as a result, I learned how *not* to take it personally.

When I was on the dating scene, I knew in my heart that I was a "catch" so if some guy out there didn't treat me with kindness or respect, I was able to pull the handle, send him down the chute and say "Next!"

He's Just Not That Into You is all about understanding the signs. For instance, when a guy doesn't call you when he says he will, he's just not that into you. Next!

If a guy doesn't call you after a date – no, he didn't lose your phone number – he's just not that into you. Next!

When a guy doesn't introduce you to his family and friends after several months of dating, he's just not that into you. Next!

When a guy doesn't put you first or ask you to marry him (after 4 years of dating, i.e., The Suit). Next!

> "If a guy wants to see you, he will see you. I once called 55 Lauren Bells until I got the right one."
> — Alex from He's Just Not That Into You (the movie)

If someone is not there for you the way you want them to be, chances are they are not *that* into you. Don't be afraid to set your standards high. Next!

Where Are Those Perfect People?

Where does one go to find love?

The first places to start revolve around things that you are passionate about. Say you have a love of home building or carpentry, you might volunteer for a Habitat for Humanity project. Or if you have always wanted to learn Italian, take a class. If you love to do yoga, you might check out a new studio. (The last yoga class I took had about 40 people in it and 35% were male!) Perhaps you find a new church or take a class on Buddhism. Think about where you can go to find people who love to do what you love to do.

The list of meeting spots for singles is a long one. Bookstores, libraries, coffee shops, bars, dance clubs, dance studios, classes, dating clubs, supper clubs, book clubs, supermarkets, gyms, golf courses, rowing clubs, dog parks, mini-putts, comedy clubs, self-improvement courses, networking groups, Toastmasters, meditation classes, yoga studios, rock climbing, volunteering, speed dating, dating services, online dating, casinos, shopping malls ... Well, you get the picture. The idea isn't to always be on the prowl, but to be open to love no matter where you are.

> *Think about where you can go to find people who love to do what you love to do.*

When you hang out in places that are known for being meat markets, you are probably not going to meet the type of people who seek long-term relationships. And if you are in your 40s for goodness' sake, stay out of the cougar bars! Yuck!

Remember my friend Kara – she's the huge adventurer – she belongs to a singles club in Toronto that organizes groups for hiking, skiing, kayaking and all kinds of fun trips. She's met a lot of really fun people.

The Soft Setup

You hear a lot of relationships beginning when a blind date is set up through a friend. A soft setup is similar but it's not really labeled a setup. You're invited out to do something with your friends and another person (who you might just click with) is also invited. There's no label like "blind date" applied. It's simply "Hey, come along bowling with us on Saturday. We have a friend Alan who we want you to meet."

If your friend knows you and knows the other person, then what have you got to lose? If they get it wrong, don't hold it against them, they were just trying to help.

Another soft tactic (like in Lisa's story) is when friends have a party, and they simply invite you both without any pressure for you to hit it off. You're just two people attending a party. Being out doing what you love is the best place to shine brightly. When you are shining, you'll be attracting – and attractive to – others.

So how can you make some of these things happen? Talk to your friends, and tell them what you're looking for. Maybe someone will pop into their minds. Or maybe they'll arrange that party and will invite a few singles for you.

> *Being out doing what you love is the best place to shine brightly. When you are shining, you'll be attracting others.*

Dating 4.0

More and more people are opting into Internet dating as it's become a very acceptable way to screen and meet new people. It can make you feel hopeful just based on the sheer volume of people available. And these days there are dating websites for every specific type of group you can imagine based on religion, sports, single parenting, age, hobbies, etc. Ask around to see what your friends have used successfully.

My experience is that most people have good intentions, but you need to go into it eyes wide open. For example, if someone won't share a photo with you relatively early on, then that may be cause for concern. There is often misrepresentation when it comes to things like height and weight criteria.

When there is an abundance of choice on your screen, you might start with the people who look most like they might be a good fit: you see some common interests, you are attracted to them physically, they say something in their profile that you connect with, or they make you laugh.

You can also narrow your search based on age and where someone lives. If you have a lot of choices, then start with the most local and work out from there.

If you know that smoking is a non-negotiable, then that makes it easier to hit "Next" when looking at a smoker. Don't think, "Oh, I can change them." For goodness' sake, just hit "Next."

Keep safety in mind at all times when Internet dating. Meet in public places where there are lots of people around. Never have someone pick you up on a first date, maybe even the second or third. Lord knows I've coffee dated a few whack jobs to whom I wished I hadn't given my phone number. For this reason, I'd probably hold off exchanging phone numbers until after the coffee date. Most people won't mind this. This is another reason why I wouldn't spend 2 months getting to know someone online.

If they insist on talking, purchase an "online phone number" very cheaply with Skype or another provider using your computer. Nowadays we have more choices. The call comes in over your computer and you can accept the call and talk to them (using your mic and speakers) or let it go to voice mail. The brilliant part is that you don't have to give out your home phone number until you are sure you really want to date a person.

Meet them face-to-face, it's the only way to know if you click.

I usually didn't "chat" online with too many people. I just felt like it was more time invested into a relationship that may or may not pan out. But you can make your own choices and decide what mediums work best. And, be aware of where you post a profile. Some sites have "intimate encounters" sections – those are people looking strictly for sex.

Again, I would not waste a lot of time talking with someone through technology (i.e., IM'ing, texting, e-mailing back and forth). Of course, there are times when it can't be helped (like long distance) but I'd avoid long-distance dating as well if possible.

Why?

The only way to tell if you have a connection, a real connection, is to get face to face. You might meet someone you've invested several months in, only to find that you don't have any chemistry with that person. (Remember Margaret's story? That's why she was so nervous!) Or the photo they sent you didn't reflect them at all.

You will continue to hear more and more success stories about people meeting online like John and I did. But that doesn't mean you don't need to keep your own personal safety in mind. If the little hairs on the back of your neck stand up, for crying out loud do some digging to make sure you're not with someone freaky or, worse, dangerous.

The Integrity Profile

When you go onto a dating website, they require some information from you to develop a profile. Most of them have check boxes for much of the criteria (physical description, likes and dislikes, activities, etc.) Those are really helpful.

But then there's always a space at the end to submit something in your own words (the essay). Here are a few basics for putting your best foot forward on your dating profile.

1. *Have Integrity:* Don't fib about anything. If you are 30 pounds overweight and there's an option between "average" and "a few extra pounds," check the second one. There's no need to mention it again in your essay.

2. *Photos:* Most sites allow you more than one photo. Make sure one is a head and shoulders shot and one is a full body

shot. You want people to know who you are and what you really look like. Glamour shots are completely bogus – don't use them. You will never look like that again in your life!

3. *Headlines Matter:* Being a marketer by profession, headlines are really important in my world. Which profile would you gravitate towards: Vivacious Divorcée Seeks Adventurer or Honest Man Wanted? The first one, perhaps?

4. *Typos:* Have someone else check your spelling and grammar. You don't want your first impression to be one that makes you look less intelligent.

5. *Hit All the Right Marks:* Tell them about yourself using interesting descriptors (intelligent, fun-loving, outgoing, curious). And describe what you are looking for (kind, generous, worldly, engaging).

6. *Don't Be Afraid to Tell Them Things that Make You Unique:* The person who is perfect for you should love you exactly as you are! (So tell them "I am a lover of nature and animals, therefore have chosen to be a vegan.") That doesn't mean you lead with your whole, sad story, if you have one. But do include anything that might be a shocker to them like a major health issue that has you in a wheelchair.

7. *Describe Your Activities:* Rather than just listing a bunch of activities (cycling, hiking), try to paint a picture of what your perfect day might look like with your ideal partner. (My perfect day involves relaxing on the beach, a bike ride, reading a good book and a homemade gourmet dinner – I'm a great cook – with a beautiful bottle of wine.)

Success Story

KAY

Who Is Mr. Right Today?

I had dated a lot since my divorce in 1994. After a long marriage, I was a different person than the girl who got married, so I wanted to date enough to figure out "Who is Mr. Right today?"

I was very open to dating lots of different types of men. I did not limit myself by age, education, income, or ... well, at 5'9", height was a consideration. While there were heartbreaks, I kept the mantra, "Each person is in your life for a reason, a season or forever."

I'd placed my profile on Match.com so I would receive their e-mails of available men. I thought it would provide a feeling of abundance; there are lots of great men out there looking for a life partner and it helped.

After several years of trial without success, Nick's profile and "e-mail alert" arrived in my mailbox. His screen name was "Curious," and his profile made me like him before I met him. The Curious name was too hard to ignore – curiosity was a big value of mine.

Nick won my heart when, after agreeing to a date the weekend after he returned from a trip to China, he called me on a Sunday morning saying, "I got home early and would love to meet for a drink this evening. But please know that I'll still want that date next weekend."

We both quit Match.com after our first date.

We've been dating nearly 2 years and we're committed to being life partners. I continue to learn about myself through challenges and joyful times, just as I learned about myself through the challenges and joys of dating in my mid-40s and 50s. Yes, I wish I'd had one for-life marriage, but that was not the road I was on. And this path is so much richer than being lonely in a marriage.

••

First Dates

Now you may be different, but I prefer the casual coffee date to anything else. First, it's short and sweet, so if the person looks 20 years older than their photo (and they lied about their age) you can have a pleasant coffee and then skedaddle.

You also avoid alcohol with this method, which can sometimes skew your view of someone. You'll have a clear mind. At a coffee shop, there is usually no waiter to interrupt. Although you do want to see how your date treats people, that can wait. Coffee dates are also cheap, so you don't feel guilty if the other person buys for you.

Girls: It's a hard thing to know who should pay on dates. My rule (and I'm not saying this is the only way to go) was that I'd let him pay for the first two dates, and then I would start sharing it back and forth (you paid for the movie, I'll get the popcorn). If he's offended by letting you pay, then that shows you something about his personality.

Also, I think it's nice to talk about it (paying) with your date so they know where you stand on it. If a guy thinks that you are going to expect him to pay for everything on every single date, he might not see you as an equal. Personally, I always wanted to weed out guys who were penny-pinchers, because that was not my style. So if they were squeamish about paying $4.00 for a coffee at Starbucks, then that told me what I needed to know. Next!

Success Story

JANE & JOHN

Meet Cute

We agreed to get together at Jack Astor's, a local restaurant, for a quick drink on Thursday after work. John and I had connected on a dating website at the beginning of the summer but nothing ever came of it. I assumed he was just another flake and moved on. But when he came back around again a few months later, I decided to give him a chance based on my philosophy of being "open to love."

Based on our earlier interaction, my expectations were not very high. I thought, "I'll get in, have one drink, and be home in time for *Grey's Anatomy.*"

But something happened.

Even though I had seen his photo, I had asked John to wait outside the restaurant. Blind dates are scary to begin with and I thought it would help ease that awkward initial "30-second search." I had occasionally approached the wrong person – "Are you Tom?" – only to feel embarrassed and stupid.

At 5:55 p.m., I drove past the restaurant and he was standing out front. Six-foot-four-inches tall, salt-and-pepper hair and a gorgeous bright smile. He saw me and waved – very friendly.

I thought to myself, "Hmmm, this might just be all right. Good thing TIVO is set to record *Grey's Anatomy.*"

He came to my car to meet me, gave me a warm hug and walked me inside. Score a point for the gentleman. He was gracious, escorting me into the bar and offering me a drink.

Having no need to assert my inner feminist (dude, I can afford my own drink), I said thank-you and ordered an Australian red.

He ordered a glass of red wine for himself as well. Score another point for the boy, a wine drinker.

After a few minutes of small talk, he just stopped with this puzzled look on his face and said genuinely, "I can't believe you've never been married before; look at you, you're gorgeous." Cha-ching, cha-ching, cha-ching. Serious point accumulation for the boy.

We moved out of the bar and into the restaurant and our 30-minute drink turned into a 4-hour dinner. We laughed and sometimes got emotional as we talked about our lives. He told me about his business, his divorce, his two daughters in college and his mom in a nursing home.

I told him about my life and my family and my career. I was myself with him. He was himself with me. We both felt calm and confident that this was something that we wanted to explore further. There were no games, no guessing, no wondering, "Does he like me? Will he call?" We both just knew.

That fall was one of the most fun, yet peaceful times, in my life. We spent weekends at my cottage at the lake, watching sunsets at the beach, drinking hot toddies in front of the campfire and sharing pieces of our lives with each other. It was magical.

Our families loved each other and us together. John's daughters, 19 and 21, were gracious in accepting me without question. They could see that their dad was happy. And it came as no surprise to anyone when we got engaged early the following year.

John proposed to me at one of our favorite restaurants right before a Barenaked Ladies concert. Even though we had talked about marriage from early on in the relationship, I sat at the concert in a state of stunned euphoria. I had always known that I would be with someone special – I knew he would be worth the wait – but after kissing so many frogs, I was really starting to wonder. It was a relief to know that he had finally come along.

The "Available" Attitude

There's a really fine line to be aware of when you are moving into this mode of attracting your perfect mate. It goes back to the energy or vibe you are putting out. Do you want to walk into a room with an attitude that screams "I'm single and I'm on the prowl" or do you want to set the energy for "I'm fabulous. Why don't you approach me and see if I'm available?"

Do you want to walk into a room with an attitude that screams "I'm single and I'm on the prowl" or do you want to set the energy for "I'm fabulous. Why don't you approach me and see if I'm available?"

My girlfriend once told me that I was so boy crazy that I didn't even see the women in the room. Wow, that was a big wake-up call for me. I had no idea I was so laser focused on men. And the vibe I put out was smacking more desperate than fabulous.

In fact, I've heard a lot of people say that it's when they are happy with their lives that love walks in the backdoor. Or perhaps they're standing in the next aisle, like Coleman was.

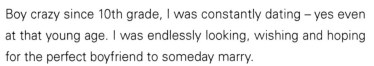

Success Story

CAROL

Love Unexpected

Boy crazy since 10th grade, I was constantly dating – yes even at that young age. I was endlessly looking, wishing and hoping for the perfect boyfriend to someday marry.

In college and beyond I had some serious relationships but not with anyone I could picture spending forever with. My theme song became, "You want to say 'I do' but I don't." The search for the right one continued.

After 5 years of teaching, I was offered a job as a professional backup singer. It was fun to sing with Roy Clark, Johnny Cash and even Mickey Dolenz of the Monkees. The travel was non-stop. And although I met many guys, it was difficult to have a real relationship from the road … and, more importantly, I felt that I wasn't living my purpose.

Fifteen years ago, I switched gears to become a full-time professional motivator. It felt so right to blend my entertainment and teaching backgrounds together – and it required less travel.

I was now past my 30s and felt abundant with my incredible family, friends, home and speaking career. Many of my best buddies were also single and we agreed that, hey, we didn't need a partner to feel complete.

Then came Coleman Murphy!

Five years ago I was in the checkout line at OfficeMax and the guy at the next counter looked a little familiar. Something made me ask if he was a guitar player. Surprised, he answered, "Yes, that's what I do full time, mostly on recording sessions."

We've never figured out where I would have seen him, but that short conversation turned into our exchange of business cards.

After a few weeks of e-mails and phone calls, we met at a local place for a glass of wine. After a few hours of conversation, we realized that we had lots in common and couldn't wait to get together again.

Three years of dating later, we got married. (Oh boy, was my mom happy.) Each day, we fall more in love than ever!

I found the love of my life when I stopped looking.

What Are Your Rules?

I am not a fan of the books that tell you to act a certain way until you've "snagged" your man. Don't kiss on the first date, that kind of stuff. I don't really believe it's about "capturing" a man; it's about two complete people coming together. So think about creating your own set of rules for dating.

You might let him take the initiative on setting up dates, for instance. That shows that he really is into you and that's cool. But don't play games or try to be someone that you're not. Be yourself.

One of my rules was no full disclosure on a first date. I didn't feel the need to "tell all" up front. Sharing all the problems you had with your newly divorced spouse is probably not going to endear people to you. Allow them to get to know you before you start in on the complicated issues. Showing up to a coffee date and displaying all of your scars and wounds may just scare them away. Start with the positive.

> But don't play games or try to be someone that you're not. Be yourself.

In the beginning of a relationship, ask yourself the really tough questions. Am I overlooking something important (i.e., he only calls me from his cell phone)? Do we share some values? Is he really into me ... *really*? Do we have a full connection, or is it just physical?

Here's what I mean by setting your own rules. These are just samples. I want you to tweak them to suit you.

After the first date: Gauge his interest. Did he show you that he was interested? Or did he play it cool? Before you go down the mental road of dating and marrying this guy, allow some time to pass before you get swept away.

Maybe your rule is "I'm not going to make a move towards him, until he shows me he is interested."

Or, maybe you're not that into him.

Maybe your rule is "I'll be open and give him a few dates to see if I missed something the first time, or to see if a spark develops over time." Practice dates can never hurt, and you're getting out of the house!

After a couple more dates: Okay, he's shown his interest. Are things moving in the right direction? Or does he keep saying he just wants to take it slow or he doesn't want to ever get married again. When someone tells you things like this you need to *listen*. Otherwise, 9 months from now you're going to be thinking marriage, and he's not heading in that direction at all. Don't be afraid to disqualify someone who doesn't want what you want. You probably *can't change him*!

So your rule? If we don't want the same things, negotiate or cut him loose.

After a few months of dating: Are you seeing him as much as you would like? If he's putting you last on his list, then girl, you have some serious thinking to do. If you're last now, you may be last forever. Personally (see the story of The Suit in Step 2) I would never put up with that again. What it really means is that you aren't *the one*. Now, this may be something that you can negotiate, but I just really want you to be aware of it.

What might your rule be? You must be very close to the top of his priority list.

After a year of dating: People say that you shouldn't make any major decisions until you're together for a year and I think it's wise. John and I moved in together after less than 6 months. That could have easily blown up in our faces, but fortunately, it worked out. If I were advising someone else, I'd say show a little patience and wait a year.

But hey, didn't I just say make up your own rules??? So you do what feels right for you. When it feels right, it feels right and that's what may drive a lot of your decisions. But if you haven't had a lot of dating experience, every guy might feel right, so be cautious.

What's your rule in this case? Check your gut. If it feels right for both of you, you might be in good shape.

You've been dating for a couple of years: Let's say you've been together more than a year and nothing is moving forward. One of the hardest things to do after you have invested a lot of time in a relationship is to cut bait and walk away. If you have a major issue (e.g., his kids are always between you, he's non-committal, you fight all the time), then you have to re-evaluate this situation.

Your rule? Express your concern, give it a few months to right itself and then be prepared to walk away.

Showing Up Fabulous

When walking into a first date, you want to really feel great about yourself. You want to show up confident, fabulous and full of life. So what's going to help you create that for yourself?

Think about wearing something casual that really makes you feel great. Check in with someone else if you're not certain if something looks good on you. Sadly, we've all seen women wearing something two sizes too small or ten years too young for their body! Don't get caught in some sort of fashion trap if it's not your style, size or isn't age appropriate.

It's a fine line between sexy and hoochie mama. Keep your intention clear.

When you look at yourself in the mirror ask yourself, "Who will I attract wearing this outfit?" If your blouse is low cut with major boobage showing, then you might just snag yourself a player who's out for a one-night stand.

But another important part of showing up fabulous is how you look (and feel) on the inside. Use your mantra going into the date. Maybe it's something like "I'm a confident woman who is a terrific catch."

I was recently coaching a 35-year-old woman who was going out for a big on-air TV job with CNN. Although a brilliant and stunning financial analyst, her confidence was sometimes sketchy. She wasn't always able to walk into interviews oozing confidence. So we set up a mantra for her that stoked her self-esteem right beforehand. Walking into that next interview she stood extremely tall (both physically and psychologically), did a great job in front of the camera and made it to the next round of auditions.

Don't Go Losing You!

If you're anything like me, you have the ability to get "swept away" by a relationship. You don't see your friends as much or do the things that you love because you want to spend time with your partner. Check out Charlotte's discovery.

 *Success Story*

CHARLOTTE

Finding Herself and Love

Before I met and married my husband I went through several failed relationships and I remember feeling like I had lost myself in the pursuit of others. One day I realized I had no interests, no hobbies, no girlfriends, no passions, no wishes/hopes/dreams, and I was miserable. I was wrapped up in waiting on whomever I was dating at the time to call.

I decided to focus on me and figure out what I liked and wanted and if a guy called, great; if not ... oh well. I lived in Minnesota at the time and it was the dead of winter when I had this epiphany. I decided to take swimming lessons and plowed through freezing temperatures to get to my lessons at the YMCA each week after work. I had forgotten about my love of theatre so I started going to every play I heard about, and even auditioned for a small part and got it (with pay). I started reading again and extending my business trips to visit places I hadn't seen before.

Then one day I realized I was giddy with joy ... because I had rediscovered *me*, and my life was full and complete, and I was completely comfortable with me. Whether someone called or not, I was not just okay, but I was good!

And then, at a party (where I was supposed to be getting set up with a guy, which didn't work) I met Ron (now my husband). Because I had a full life I wasn't desperate. We dated for 5 years before marrying, and celebrated our 21st anniversary last August. I had a relapse during those 5 years (waiting for him to call, losing myself in him, etc.) but then I had to snap back and remember what I had done before meeting him. I think when he saw that I had a life and it was going to go on with or without him, he decided to propose.

Bottom line: my inner work was rediscovering me.

⋯⋯⋯⋯⋯⋯⋯⋯⋯⋯⋯⋯⋯⋯⋯⋯⋯⋯⋯⋯⋯⋯⋯⋯⋯⋯⋯⋯

Well, I now believe not losing yourself is all about balance and maintaining a strong identity. By failing to do things that make you feel good, you are undermining your relationship. And please note that if someone is isolating you from your friends and family, you have a big problem. That is not a healthy relationship. It's one of control.

Creating balance in your relationship means that you might put them first, but do not drop everything else from your list. I believe that in many marriages "the couple" takes whatever time is leftover after all of the activities are scheduled in. It's no wonder so many relationships fail. Women, especially mothers, often don't leave any room for themselves in the schedule. Not even time for a bubble bath. And then 10 years later, they try to figure out what went wrong. What went wrong is that they lost themselves in their family and in their kids. They must put themselves at the top of the list.

Easier said than done, I know. One of the main things that I associated with relationships was "loss of freedom" which is why it took so darn long for me to commit. What I realized was that I could be in a relationship and still have freedom – still take time for myself. And I do. I go to the gym, take my mom to the movies and take bubble baths several times a week. Maybe you can't afford as much time as I can, but what can you do to take care of yourself? What can you do when you are in a relationship to ensure that you don't lose yourself?

One of my favorite books on dating is *If the Buddha Dated* by Charlotte Kasl. In it she writes, "Differentiation means the ability to maintain your identity when you are in close relationship to other people or ideologies: you are able to rest securely inside yourself and not be swept away by other people's emotions, opinions, or moods."

While starting onto the dating scene, it's good to remind yourself to stay true to you.

When you first get into a relationship, establishing your own feelings about the topics of life is important – and maintaining your values and opinions is equally important. Remember Julia Roberts' character in *The Runaway Bride*? She didn't know what kind of eggs she liked for breakfast. Why? Because she always took on her partners' likes and dislikes. With one man it was scrambled, another sunny side up, another poached. She was always losing herself and that's why instinctively she would run away – for survival. She had to find herself – and keep herself – before she could find true love.

Practice Boyfriends

Remember The Fishmonger at the beginning of the book? He was an amazing practice boyfriend who really helped me open up to the idea of love. He didn't turn out to be "the one" but I saw major value in our time together.

There was another one ... The Ballplayer.

Frog Story
THE BALLPLAYER

When I was in my 20s, I was bartending and waitressing at a sports bar and had a lot of opportunity to meet men. Some of my regulars were a group of mostly single, semi-pro ballplayers so it was inevitable that I would date a couple of them.

The first one I chose was your typical "player" named Alex. He was good looking and cocky and bit of a jerk. I dated him for a couple of weeks and then realized that it wasn't going to work. He was just too into himself.

A couple of months after we broke up I noticed his friend Todd. Todd was the polar opposite of Alex. He was shy, sweet and cute, in his own more conservative way. And damn if he didn't look hot in those tight baseball pants. This was a big turning point for me, because I had traded a good-looking jerk for a nice guy! I had never done that before.

Todd and I ended up dating for a year. He was the first long-term relationship I'd had where I felt valued and appreciated. He treated me with respect, we communicated well and rarely argued, and had a great time together. He opened doors for me, took me out to nice dinners (lots of times I paid because I made good money), sent me flowers and showed me what a real relationship looked like.

> *This was a big turning point for me, because I had traded a good-looking jerk for a nice guy! I had never done that before.*

But there was something missing.

I knew all along that I wasn't going to marry Todd. I was much more ambitious than he was. And although I loved him, I didn't feel like he was "the one." There was a medium-sized spark, but I wanted something that sizzled. He was sweet but I knew that I wanted to travel and do more with my life before settling down. It was hard to let this one go, though. How would I know if another one like him would come along?

But I did. I ended up leaving our relationship behind and moved to Australia for a year. I never did regret it. He was a great practice boyfriend.

Lessons from the Frog

The Ballplayer was a good lesson in not settling. Marriage was tempting because we were so comfortable and we did "love" each other, but we didn't have the spark that I knew we should have. There was no va-va-voom.

He also showed me what a great relationship should look like. Knowing how you want to be treated is difficult if you don't have anything to compare it to. In this relationship I was able to discover how I wanted to be treated and from then forward I never really settled for anything less.

Of course, I have the luxury of hindsight on this one. If I had married The Ballplayer, I would have stayed in that small town and probably had babies. I would have never lived in Australia, or Dallas or Vancouver or Calgary. And I might not have been free to end up in my hometown when my parents needed me.

Staying After Practice

The danger with the practice boyfriend ... staying long after practice is over. I could have easily gone back to The Ballplayer after Australia, but I didn't want to rest on a relationship that lacked sizzle.

It's easy to get into a comfortable routine with someone who is good to you. But I really want to encourage you to go for the whole enchilada! The entire package. The spark, the shared values and the friendship! If you marry for security or to have someone to take care of you, you may just find yourself in a relationship with a controller. (I'm not a therapist, but I can certainly see where marrying for the wrong reasons can turn into a nightmare.)

Red Flags

I think that people in relationships sometimes find themselves wondering, "Is this normal?" Maybe they feel nervous around their spouse because they have an explosive temper, maybe their partner doesn't talk to them for days because of an argument, maybe they haven't had sex in weeks or months. I know that when you get married young and fall into these less-than-satisfying situations, you don't figure out how much dysfunction you're living with until you are out of the relationship.

My friend Joanne said that when she left her marriage she felt lighter and people were noticing a huge difference in her. She had no idea that the weight of her marriage – constantly walking on eggshells to avoid a conflict with her spouse – was showing up on her face.

If you can be clear on what you want from a relationship going into it, then you'll be better able to gauge how it's going when you're in the thick of things. I remember once thinking in the middle of a heated argument with a boyfriend, "This isn't me. I'm not a yeller." But it wasn't until I was clear on what a good relationship looked like that I could walk away from the ones that weren't good.

When you date for a couple of decades you pick up a tip or two about how to see red flags very early on. What are some red flags you should be looking for when first getting involved with someone?

1. Doesn't treat you with respect.
2. Doesn't treat others well (like restaurant servers).
3. Drives like a madman (road rage).
4. Has a super close relationship with his mother (sorry girls, you might think this is sweet, but it's going to cause you problems).
5. Let's his kids walk all over him. (Different values around raising kids is a huge problem – just watch *Dr. Phil* a time or two. It's an epidemic.)
6. Spends too much or too little money.
7. Controlling. Wants to keep you all to himself; isolates you from everyone; is highly jealous. Don't be fooled into thinking, "Well it's just his way of showing me he loves me." This is a *big red flag*!

8. Quick to anger. Any sign of violence what so ever is a *big red flag.*

9. Judgmental, overly critical of others, racist, prejudiced.

10. Drinks or eats too much or has any other addiction. Recovering addicts are also a little tricky. Be sure you know what you are signing up for.

11. Financial problems? You should know relatively early on whether or not someone has a huge debt load. *Big red flag.*

12. Needs saving. If you keep thinking, "I can help them with that" or "I can fix that," don't delude yourself.

13. Married. Just walk away.

Ah, yes, number 13. That's right; I've mentioned this one a couple of times. This one is absolutely non-negotiable. I should really confess that I learned this one the hard way.

Frog Story

THE HOCKEY JOCK

In my early days working at the sports bar, we had a new AHL hockey team move into the arena next door. We got to know the team pretty well as they became regulars at the bar after games.

They'd all walk in wearing their expensive suits, looking pretty fine, but I had a "no hockey player" policy. We called them "hockey pucks," and their groupies "puck bunnies." And I didn't think many of them could be trusted, if any. Most of these kids were youngsters heading up to the NHL, and since I was in my mid-20s, my policy was pretty firm.

But after a few months, one of the management caught my eye. He was a former player and now the trainer for the team. He was stocky, with a mean set of hockey legs (they were hard to resist) and chiseled face. He wasn't walking-down-the-street-knock-you-over handsome; he was more the type that you noticed over time. And he was funny. Funny has always been attractive to me. He was in his mid-30s so not nearly as green as the kids he worked with.

Over the course of a few months, he came into the bar and would flirt with me and make me laugh. We had a really great connection and I was becoming interested, despite my "no hockey puck" policy. Things heated up and we started going out together. He'd come by the bar and wait for me to finish my shift. We'd go back to my place or out for a drink next door. He lived out of town, so he stayed over once in awhile.

My boss and fellow servers (who were my best friends) could see I was falling for him. But none of us really knew The Hockey Jock that well and we were in for a shock.

One afternoon, the bar was slow and my boss was catching up with the local paper and relaying some of the stories to me. "Here's one about the Oilers," he said. The boys from the AHL team were mentioned constantly and a story about them wasn't unusual. But then I heard, "Uh oh!"

"What?" I said.

"Ahhhhh, not sure you want to see this?"

"What? Tell me!" I repeated. He pointed to the article that talked about my boyfriend and *his wife*!!!

"What!?! He's married! That son of a bitch. I'll kill him!" There aren't enough expletives to describe how I took this news.

I was angry and in shock. I had no idea what was going on in the other half of this guy's life. I felt like a complete and utter fool. My boss was really upset to be the one to bear this bad news, but I needed to know. I think we all felt a little duped!

The Hockey Jock was lucky that my boss was able to warn him before I got to him the next time he dropped into the bar. To say I was pissed was an understatement. I was furious!

But when I calmed down and thought it through I realized how young and stupid I had been. I had never asked if he was married. I just assumed because he didn't wear a wedding ring that he wasn't – DUH!!! I had never asked for his home phone number. In fact, I was just having a good time and asked very few questions. I didn't leave him totally blameless. In my mind he was a rotten cheating bastard, but I took on some of the responsibility for the situation too.

I moped around that bar for months and fortunately he had the good sense to stay away. He did try to come back around once to try to patch things up. "Are you kidding? You're married!" I said.

And I kicked his sorry ass out of that bar. Big lesson!

Lessons from the Frog

Oh boy, where do I begin? No matter your age, don't be naïve like I was. I'm pretty sure this changed who I was as a person. I was quite bitter about men for awhile. But taking some of the responsibility allowed me to learn the lesson and move forward. I've always resisted being a victim and you should too. I chose badly and it turned out badly. Next time, I knew to ask a few more questions.

Be on the lookout for red flags. If he doesn't give you his home phone number, you've never been to his place, you don't go out in public a great deal – something's up.

What If They Are Married?

My best advice if you get tangled up with a married man is to head for the hills. Let's say you meet a guy at work and he's great. You laugh together and flirt, and he really seems to "get" you. He shares with you that he's into you, but that he's married. He's not happy in his marriage but he has kids, blah, blah, blah. What do you do?

Here's the conversation with the Married Guy (MG) …

MG: I'm really into you. Why don't we get together for a drink sometime?

You: Really, you're into me?

MG: Yeah, look at you. You're totally hot and fun to be around.

You: Ah, that's so sweet. (You're soaking this up purely for self-esteem purposes.)

MG: So what about that drink?

You: But what about your wife?

MG: Well, we have an arrangement.

You: Oh, really?

MG: Yeah, she kind of does her thing, and I kind of do mine.

You: So, if I talked to your wife at the next office party, would she confirm this?

MG: (Sensing a change, starts to waffle.) Uhhhhh …
    (Note: Even if he tries to bullshit his way through this, don't fall for it.)

You: I'll tell you what. I'll stay single, and you stay married, and if that situation ever changes, like you get divorced, we'll talk, okay?

MG: (Stunned silence.)

Ladies, until they *aren't* married, they *are* married. Run, run, very fast in the other direction! Men do leave their wives more now than they did in the olden days, but hooking up with a married man is just asking for a shit storm to rain down on your head.

When you date a married man think about this. Your relationship will have started under ugly circumstances. You will not be proud of your behavior. You will not enjoy hurting all of the people in his life (and possibly his kids). You will not enjoy being "the other woman" and hearing the gossip that will follow you both around for years to come. And remember this … if he cheated on his wife with you, what's to say he won't cheat on you someday. If you fall in love with the wrong person, my advice is to wait it out.

Even if a man does leave his marriage, there's no guarantee he's not going to want some freedom. Keep living your life until you are sure that he is available both physically and emotionally.

Relationships that Stand the Test of Time

We hear and read a lot about couples who have been together for long periods of time. My parents have been married for more than 60 years. It's so amazing and so foreign to me. Sometimes I'll be in another room and I'll hear them talking quietly and laughing together. After 60 years, how cute is that?

When asked, many couples say that communication has been the key to their relationship longevity; some cite laughter; others say "never go to bed angry."

I saw Goldie Hawn talking about her relationship with Kurt Russell and she said, "He constantly challenges my mind." We really have to think about our growth when selecting our partner. Will he or she help us get to where we want to go in our lives?

What I think is difficult to predict is how you will grow as a person. If you marry young, the odds that you will outgrow your partner or start to want different things in life go up. This is where we fall back on our values. Even though I might go off on a spiritual quest (that John doesn't participate in), I'm hoping that our shared values and love of doing the same things day to day will be the glue that keeps us together. If he hated travel and I thought I was never going to get to see the places on my bucket list, we'd have some serious issues. I was very clear that a big part of seeking a partner was to experience the world with someone.

We really have to think about our growth when selecting our partner. Will he or she help us get to where we want to go in our lives?

If you get anything out of this book, I hope it will be that your choice of partner is so important. I really hope you don't settle for someone just for the sake of getting married or playing house. Some people marry for money and they pay for it every day of their lives. I want you to want the most and the best for yourself. Because when you get it, it will have been worth the wait.

The Relationship Fitness Test

Whether you are looking back on a previous relationship, or something more current, here are some signs that will tell you whether or not you are in a mature and healthy relationship. If your current relationship doesn't have many of the items on this list, you may want to reassess or get to work on changing the relationship.

- *Respect.* You both respect each other and speak kindly of the other, even when the other is not in the room.
- *Fun.* You have fun together and you laugh often.

- *Commitment*. You are in it for the long haul – no ifs, ands, or buts about it. It's a done deal and you are both very clear on this. (Note: If you are in the early stages, this may need to wait until you are both ready.)

- *Trust*. You know without a doubt that you are both faithful and committed to the success of the relationship. You not only trust them to be faithful, but to move through life with the best interest of the relationship in mind.

- *Shared Values*. You value the same things in life, i.e., honesty, family and friends, adventure, nature, money. (See more on this in Step 1.)

- *Individuality*. You came into the relationship as individuals and continue to maintain your own identity, activities, friends and interests.

- *Communication*. You handle difficult situations by talking them through, each person feeling as though they have been heard.

- *Best Friend*. You always have a shoulder to lean on when times are tough, a best friend who is on your side.

- *Intimacy*. You feel connected to one another, even when you are apart. You enjoy intimate moments as well as a healthy sex life.

- *Shared Vision*. You both want the same things in life, i.e., home, children, travel, early retirement, security.

- *You Are Better*. Your partner makes you want to be a better person – a sure sign that you are in a healthy relationship. When you look forward and see yourself doing everything that you want in life with this person – without limitations – you are in a healthy relationship.

Ideas to Ponder

Leaping into the dating world is scary. Putting yourself out there can be daunting. But knowing that you are fabulous and in a happy place with yourself is the first step. Having some tools and "rules" is the final step.

- If you like to cook, doesn't it make sense that other people who like to cook will also be at a cooking class? Identify some of the things you like to do, that make you happy, that you enjoy. Then go do them. Sign up for a class, join a club, whatever will get you to places where there will be other people who also like those activities.

- Is Internet dating the new singles club? It can be, but there are lots of great sites out there. You need to look them over carefully, keeping safety in mind, and have some fun with it.

- How can you still be you and enjoy your new relationship? How will you create balance and not lose yourself?

- Create your list of red flags. While you don't want to concentrate on the negative, you do need to know what you do *not* want in a partner. What is unacceptable to you?

Now, Leap!

So now you know the approach for becoming a Frog Whisperer. It's not that complicated; it just takes some work and a plan, like anything worthwhile. You need to decide what it is that you really want – get READY. Then become the best version of yourself and resolve any issues holding you back – get SET. And finally you need to get out there and whisper to a few frogs – LEAP. And before you know it, you'll have found your perfect mate!

HOME: *Jane and John Today*

As I prepare for our fourth Christmas together, I feel more sturdy, more content and happier in our relationship than ever. I think I spent a lot of year one being afraid that things were going to fall apart. Or that I would lose John. He had a heart attack when he was in his mid-40s and although it was years ago, I still worry.

Married life came easier to me than I thought would be possible. My 40-some years of singledom seemed to prepare me for what was ahead. I'd always balked at traditional roles in marriage where cooking, cleaning and laundry land on the woman's shoulders. So we have a really great balance between us and share in everything and I'm so grateful to have an evolved man.

John and I work hard, but we play hard as well. We spend our summers at the lake, usually at the beach with our Labradoodle, Molly. We enjoy a lot of downtime but by the same token, we get things done. We're a terrific team when it comes to projects. (And believe it or not, I'm pretty handy with a power drill!)

Our home is really awesome and we continue to make it our haven. We travel quite frequently but love to come home just as much. We built a stone fire pit in our backyard and spend many evenings enjoying the river with our fun-loving neighbors-turned-friends.

We go south frequently during the Canadian winters. Sometimes I think we'll buy a place in a sunny state and play golf all winter. Our bucket list is pretty long and has a few big trips, including Australia and Europe.

We are grandparents to Jayden who is now 4 and a joy. My stepdaughters have grown into beautiful and responsible young adults who are thriving. Katie, a single mom, is finishing school and works nearly full time while doing so. I don't know how she does it! Emily, a nurse, just bought a home with her boyfriend who we hope will someday become our son-in-law. She hopes to travel on humanitarian nursing missions, which, no doubt, she will do.

We are the modern-day blended family. Each year, John's ex-wife and her entire family come over for our grandson's birthday. We all get along very well and come together whenever one of our daughters needs us. I feel as though they are our extended family and our girls never have to worry about feeling torn between parents.

This past year was tough when we lost my brother Cliff and our brother-in-law Tim. Both were young and their deaths were very sudden. It was a year of loss for our families, but we made it through and I think we work well as a team when the chips are down.

Retirement is still a ways away for us, but I can see that we enjoy so many of the same things that we're going to have a really great time of it. In general, I can highly recommend married life. Of course, it's not without bumps along the way, but when I look at the alternative (which is viewing the wonders of the world by myself), I choose marriage.

I'm not naïve enough to think that we've got it made in the shade, so I do hope you'll send us some positive thoughts and prayers for a long and happy marriage. And more importantly, I hope that this book has provided you with some tools to make this happen for yourself!

Ready, Set, Leap!!!

PS: Sharin' the Love!!

We'd like to hear your story
at *www.frogwhisperer.com*!

Stop by and read the Frog Blog to keep on top
of the newest ideas in finding lasting love.

And if you found it helpful, please send your
friends to *www.frogwhisperer.com* and recommend
us on Facebook (search The Frog Whisperer).

About the Author

In September of 2007, at age 43, Jane Atkinson married John Fones in the backyard of their dream home. She is the stepmom to two beautiful daughters in their 20s (Katie and Emily) and a G-Ma to 4-year-old Jayden.

Before returning to her hometown, to be closer to her parents, Jane traveled the world and has lived in Sydney, Dallas, Vancouver, Calgary, Banff and Halifax. Prior to starting her own business, she worked at jobs ranging from deckhand on a fishing trawler to drink hostess on a cruise ship to marketing coordinator at a ski resort.

Later Jane went on to become an agent for professional speakers and has been in that field for nearly 20 years. Today, Jane owns a coaching and consulting company called Speaker Launcher that helps professional speakers catapult their careers. Her first book, *The Wealthy Speaker*, has been called "the bible" by thousands of aspiring and professional speakers.

Currently, Jane and John live in London, Ontario, Canada, with their dog, Molly, and their cat, Sweetpea. They are 55 minutes from their retreat on Lake Huron where they spend weekends in the spring, summer and fall. They hope to someday have a place in the sunny south for the winters.

For more tips on finding the mate perfect for you, or to order additional products, go to *www.frogwhisperer.com*.

CPSIA information can be obtained at www.ICGtesting.com
Printed in the USA
LVOW060400211111

255818LV00003B/6/P